Scotland's Stations

WEMYSS BAY

abellio

Northern Books
from Famedram

Thanks to . . .

Scotland's Stations first appeared in 1989, quickly followed by a second, slightly revised edition. Like the first edition, this extensively re-jigged edition owes much to the inspiration of the distinguished industrial archaeologist, Professor John Hume, who also provided many of the black and white photographs in the first edition, some of which also appear in these pages.

Thanks are also due to those stout defenders of all things rail-ish, John and Hege Barnes of Glenfinnan, whose station restoration and ongoing development there is an example to us all. Thanks are due also to those others who have worked to save the fabric of many of Scotland's stations and find new uses for them. Well done!

The first editions of this title were printed in-house in somewhat challenging mono. That was before we discovered Ajay, the guiding force behind Imprint Digital. His dedication to quality speaks for itself.

ISBN 978 0905 489 971
© 2017 Famedram Publishers Limited
Strictly no reproduction without written permission.
Published by Famedram Publishers Limited, PO Box 3, Ellon, AB41 9EA
www.northernbooks.co.uk
Print: Imprint Digital

Cover: Broughty Ferry Station. Overleaf: Wemyss Bay Station, Ayrshire. (Photograph: Frances Anderson)

Scotland's Stations

A Traveller's Guide

Northern Books

from Famedram

The Stations

Aberdeen
Aberdour
Achanalt
Achnasheen
Achnashellach
Alness
Altnabreac
Arbroath
Ardgay
Ardlui
Arisaig
Attadale
Aviemore
Ayr

Balloch
Banavie
Berwick-
   upon-Tweed
Blair Atholl
Boat of Garten
Bridge of Orchy
Brora
Broughty Ferry
Burntisland

Carnoustie
Carrbridge
Carstairs
Corpach
Corrour
Crianlarich
Culrain
Cupar

Dalmally
Dalmeny
Dalwhinnie
Dingwall
Drem
Dumbarton
   Central
Dumfries

Dunbar
Duncraig
Dundee
Dunkeld
Dunrobin

Edinburgh
   Wavereley
Elgin

Falkirk
Fearn
Forsinard
Fort William

Garve
Georgemas
   Junction
Glasgow
   Central
Glasgow
   Queen St
Glencarron
Gleneagles
Glenfinnan

Haymarket
Helmsdale
Huntly

Insch
Invergordon
Inverkeithing
Inverness
Invershin
Inverurie

Keith
Kildonan
Kinbrace
Kinghorn
Kingussie
Kyle of Lochalsh

Ladybank
Lairg
Larbert
Leuchars
Linlithgow
Lochailort
Lockerbie

Mallaig
Markinch
Morar

Nairn
Newtonmore
North Berwick

Oban

Perth
Pitlochry
Plockton

Rannoch
Rogart

Scotscalder
Spean Bridge
Stirling
Strathcarron
Stromeferry

Tain
Taynuilt
Thurso
Tulloch
Tweedbank
Tyndrum
   Lower

Upper Tyndrum

Wemyss Bay

Wick

The Story – so far

WHEN THE FIRST edition of Scotland's Stations appeared – quite a number of years ago – it was followed very promptly by an updated edition. The next update has taken rather longer and in that time much has changed.

For most people, privatisation of our railways has been little short of a disaster. Sleeper services to the North were saved after a struggle and the Forth Bridge finally got the paint job it so desperately needed – contrary to the bland re-assurances of Railtrack – but Scotland ended up with what some cruel critics have called a 'Mickey Mouse' operation based on 'guided buses' – the diesel multiple units optimistically referred to as 'Sprinters.'

The bricks and mortar – or stone and slate – fabric of Scotland's stations has fared little better. As we refer to on many occasions in this guide, the formerly rather grand railway hotels – the British Transport Hotels – were amongst the first assets to be sold off. In not a few cases they were really integral to the stations they adjoined and served. The old, magnificent North British in Edinburgh *(left)* and the Central in Glasgow are prime examples, but Perth and Aberdeen's Station Hotels were equally regrettable losses.

Even Kyle of Lochalsh had to say goodbye to its imposing Lochalsh Hotel.

But at least the hotels weren't demolished. This, alas, was the fate that befell many of the lesser known, vernacular stations in the more remote areas of the land.

Recent years have witnessed a more enlightened attitude, with the community being invited to get involved and new uses being found for redundant station buildings. A shining example in Scotland has been the Glenfinnan station complex which has gone from strength to strength over the years. Starting first as a visitor centre/museum in the

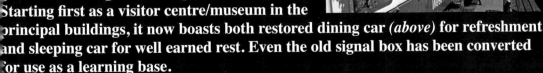

principal buildings, it now boasts both restored dining car *(above)* for refreshment and sleeping car for well earned rest. Even the old signal box has been converted for use as a learning base.

Rogart *(left)* on the Far North Line has seen equally forceful advocacy for bringing new life to old lines. Though the station itself is, as they say, 'unstaffed' a warm welcome awaits summer visitors who want to take advantage of the facilities offered by the 'Sleeperzzz' initiative offered in converted

life to the station, creating a small historical feature and turning the handsome, but disused, stationmaster's house *(below)* into a four bedroom self catering

establishment, with special discounts for those who are prepared to help keep the station tidy and for those who arrive by train – or bike.

Dumfries, a past winner of Best Station and also a finalist in the Best Station Garden competition, boasts a whole number of attractive outdoor touches on any spare station land, while the former news kiosk situated on Platform 2 has found a new life displaying railway memorabilia under the banner Railway Reflections.

Ladybank has nurtured a variety of arts ventures in its appropriately rather grand Italianate former station buildings. An earlier use of the old refreshment room was as a local ambulance base.

This more positive approach, plus a recognition of the architectural worth of many older station buildings, has had the effect of generally halting the wave of demolition that took place in earlier years, but too many rural stations still lack any sign of life. With a very few exceptions, the station bookstalls have shut up shop and all too often the cafés have closed down too.

With the railway system broken up as it is into a hundred different parts it is difficult to promote a co-ordinated approach, but they do things better on some foreign shores. What about a ticketing, tourist information presence that also offers drinks and light refreshments together with a small retail operation – rather on the lines of even the smallest filling stations? It needs joined up thinking, but it can be done – and is done in some European countries.

This guide does not pretend to be a comprehensive catalogue of all the stations in Scotland. The main city stations apart, there is a strong bias towards the weirder and wackier outposts of the system...

Stations like the ultra remote Corrour *(right),* not accessible by public road but despite this, surprisingly popular, as the Office of Rail and Road ticket sales figures would seem to suggest. Taking advantage of the limited seating facility on the early morning sleeper bound for Fort William (and back at the end of the day) a full day's hill walking can be enjoyed in this area, if not until

restaurant than had often operated in the past and it can make for a splendid day out.

Neighbouring Rannoch, though possibly not quite so remote – it can be reached down a 20 mile single track road from the metropolis of Kinloch Rannoch – offers a highly informative interpretive feature in a former waiting room (*left*) and a truly splendid tearoom serving delicious home made fare. (Whatever happened to the celebrated – or infamous – British Rail sandwich?)

At the northern extremities of the system no such luxuries exist. Indeed one is bound to wonder quite why some stations are there at all. Altnabreac (station code ABC) is really at the back of beyond and it seems it always was so. There was a hotel nearby once upon a time, but the station was there before it. Likewise a school, both long since closed.

At least annual passenger figures for Altnabreac creep into the hundreds. At Kildonan (*pictured right*), a few stops down the line towards Helmsdale, there have been years when fewer than a hundred passengers have alighted or descended from the passing trains all year. But at least Kildonan could claim there was once gold, if not in 'them thar hills', in the tumbling Kildonan burn.

It's not all doom and gloom, though. The new Borders railway, which

follows the old Waverley line to Galashiels and just beyond, has seen the opening of a number of new stations – including the new 'terminus' of Tweedbank which boasts a very sizeable car park full to the brim most days with Edinburgh bound commuters' cars. Sadly the opportunity to grace the line with some inspired 21st century station building, however modest, has been passed over. At this rate, a 22nd century edition of this guide will have very little fine architecture to record for our time!

A competition to design a modern day passenger refuge might have produced something a little more inspiring than the ubiquitous bus shelter – like the one which effectively comprises today's Galashiels 'station' – shown above.

Aberdeen

Union Square, a major shopping complex, has virtually devoured the station which now seems almost to have become a part of it. Together with other retail developments, this has damaged the city's traditional heart. Escape the retail heaven and you will still find the harbour area busy with some offshore oil activity plus an overnight ferry service to Orkney and Shetland.

Also worth seeing: Refurbished Art Gallery (good cards and local books in shop); St Machar's Cathedral and Brig o'Balgownie in Old Aberdeen – what's left of it (2/3 miles N); the old seatown – Footdee (Fittie); numerous parks throughout the city – Aberdeen is all-time outright winner of Britain in Bloom competition.

Railwayana

Opened as Joint Station by the Scottish North Eastern and the Great North of Scotland Railways, November 4 1867. Originally two stations, Guild Street and the Waterloo half a mile apart – connected by a horse-operated line for goods. Passengers were ferried to and fro by horse drawn vans.

New travel centre opened 1978 replacing old panelled booking office, which left some old woodwork still to be seen in the ladies waiting room. A further (and more tasteful) re-fit took place in the mid-eighties, followed by further very major re-modelling as a result of the Union Square upheaval. One result of this was a much less user friendly drop off arrangement for private cars, though the £2 'fine' introduced at some airports (including Aberdeen) was yet to be instituted.

Nearby Station Hotel — acquired by GNSR in 1910 and latterly a British Transport Hotel — was sold off early in the rail privatisation process.

Distances

Inverness 108 miles; Perth 92 miles; Glasgow, Queen Street 155 miles; Edinburgh, Waverley 130 miles; London, King's Cross 524 miles

ABERDOUR
KY3 0SN (Fife)

Guidelines

Today's commuter land was popular with trippers last century. Free-booting excursion steamers plied the Forth trying to beat the Forbes-Mackenzie Act, Scotland's first serious shot at anti-drink legislation.

St Fillan's Church dates from early C12, restored and rebuilt in 1926, Norman windows and all. Aberdour Castle (C14) can be seen from the line in a wooded ravine. Inchcolm Island one and a half mile trip in a motor boat from the Silver Sands.

Freshly baked morning rolls may be had from baker by station approach.

Railwayana

Opened by the NB June 2 1890. Two platforms and footbridge served by delightful 1890 stone building with ornamental barge boards and terra cotta ridge tiles.

Booking hall renowned for its floral display, complete with collecting can (an oil drum) for donations to the "Aberdour Station Garden Fund" — "A Coin a Day Keeps the Greenfly away".

Virtually on the platform itself a smart new greenhouse, *(see left)*, while on the opposite side an elaborate planted goods barrow has been seen.

Closed to goods May, '64.

Distances

Edinburgh, Waverley 17 miles; Dundee 42 miles

ACHANALT
IV23 2QD (Highland)

Guidelines
Half-way house on the Kyle line, but little to recommend it unless you are into farming! Station — or what there is of it — is reached via a farmyard. Public phone on the main road, but for how long?

On a nearby hillside, in the Cnoc na Bain Burial Ground, is the grave of the pioneer aviator Captain Bertram Dickson, famed as the first licensed airman in Scotland.

Railwayana
Opened by Dingwall and Skye Railway August 10 1870, the original building — a wooden shed — was 'consumed by fire' on December 5 1889. Today the only apparent 'station' building is a shed made from concrete blocks, the more permanent structure having become a private house. The stationmaster caused an upset in June 1879 when he set the points wrongly.

Distances
Inverness 40 miles; Kyle of Lochalsh 42 miles; Achnasheen 6 miles.

ACHNASHEEN
IV22 2EJ (Highland)

Guidelines
One time oasis on the Kyle line, formerly offering the widest range of facilities to the traveller. Hotel built originally by the railway company (but subsequently turned over to civilian management) was on the platform itself. You got a close-up of the morning train, as the dining room gave right on to the platform.

During the 70's Klondyke oil boom the public bar was a favourite stopping place for construction workers en route to or from the Howard-Doris platform building yard at Kishorn.

Nearby were craftshop, café and jewellery workshop, also PO with postbus service (yes!) to Kinlochewe, Gairloch, Poolewe, Aultbea and Laide. Alas, the hotel burnt down and was demolished and over the years, post office, café and workshop have all closed. About the only facility left (and a welcome one) is a public loo on the station itself, though the café has shown signs of a possible return to life.

Rumour has it that there are (very) occasional bus services to Poolewe(?) If you get the chance, ask for Inverewe gardens, founded by Osgood Mackenzie in 1862 and handed over to the National Trust for Scotland by his daughter in 1952. 100,000 visitors plus a year come to inspect the exotic trees and shrubs which now flourish 'where once one lone dwarf willow grew on a barren promontory'.

Railwayana
Opened by Dingwall and Skye Railway August 10 1870. Station has two platforms linked by interesting cast and wrought iron footbridge. Charming wooden goods shed *(see picture top left)* a victim of the BR demolition squad — a sad loss.

Hotel *(seen left from the air, pre-fire)* designed by Alexander Ross of Inverness in 1871. In early days of hotel operation, the Highland Railway was required by the local medical officer of health to spend nearly £100 on a new byre to separate its herd of cattle from its guests!

Distances
Inverness 46 miles; Kyle of Lochalsh 36 miles; Dingwall 26 miles.

Achnasheen

ACHNASHELLACH
IV54 8YH (Highland)

Guidelines
In midst of Achnashellach Forest and at the end of a private road helpfully 'closed to all vehicles.' Devoid of buildings apart from the ubiquitous block-work shelter, though at one stage it boasted a wooden structure bizarrely claiming allegiance to Newtonmore *(see lower picture, opposite)*. Public phone on road.

     Sturdy Achnashellach independent hostel (not part of YH scheme) 2 miles E along the road. Open all year, hostel store sells foodstuffs.

Railwayana
Opened by Dingwall & Skye Railway August 10 1870, the station has one platform. At first it was manned only during the summer months with the stationmaster sleeping in the booking office. Plans to provide a two-roomed cottage adjoining booking office fell through when the local laird refused to contribute to cost.

     On October 14 1892 a hilarious runaway train sequence ended in minor disaster when the engine which had set out in pursuit of the runaway coaches, crashed into them on the rebound!

     Closed to goods traffic on June 27 1964.

Distances
Inverness 59 miles; Kyle of Lochalsh 23 miles.

cene. Alness station re-opened in 1973 in response to boom conditions along the Cromarty Firth. That bubble soon burst and unemployment crept back.

Surprising range of shops. Large new secondary school. Nearby are Dalmore and Teaninich distilleries — always worth a visit, but wise to check first

Railwayana

Opened by Inverness & Aberdeen Junction Railway on March 21 1863, with three platforms now reduced to one.

The original elegant stone building, probably designed by Alexander Ross Inverness, was first boarded up with corrugated iron painted white to make it loo like a faded tropical outpost and then eventually unceremoniously demolished, to be replaced by the ubiquitous bus shelter.

Closed to passengers June 13 1960 and re-opened May 7 1973. For a while two rival station signs (*see left*) competed for the travellers' attention on the platform! Tickets were at one stage sold from a portakabin, leaving passengers to stand under a small awning. Now, like so many of Scotland's stations, it is unsurprisingly 'Unstaffed,' but you can always stand (or sit!) in the bus shelter.

Distances

Inverness 28 miles; Wick 133 miles; Thurso 125 miles

ALTNABREAC
KW12 6UR (Highland)

Guidelines
After Corrour, in the middle of Rannoch Moor, probably the most inaccessible station on the whole network. In the midst of a 21,000 acre peat moss with nothing for miles and only very poor access by (bumpy) road.

      Once, incongruously, the Loch Dhu Hotel stood nearby in the middle of the moor, but this closed its doors in the early 80s to become a private house. Thirty years earlier the North of Scotland Hydro Electric Board experimented hereabouts with a peat-fired power station, for which some 3000 tons of the dusky substance were gathered. Alas, the experiment ended in 1960, to be replaced today by a multitude of subsidy grabbing, short lived windmills – some even reputed to be second hand cast offs from Germany.

      In the 70s large tracts were given over to tax-dodging forestry, a popular ruse with high rollers, though less so with environmentalists.

Railwayana
Opened Sutherland and Caithness Railway July 28 1874. Once plain, but elegant station building (cost: £569) derelict by early 80s, but subsequently revived as a private house, with a ruined water tower still standing nearby. Ready for the return of steam?

Distances
Inverness 134 miles; Wick 27 miles; Thurso 19 miles.

ARBROATH
DD11 1RQ (Angus)

Guidelines
Arbroath (formerly Aberbrothock) is the home of the smokie — on sale in plenty of shops. Fish tied tail to tail, not split open like finnan haddie, and gently smoked over beech or oak chip fires.

Smokies make a fine high tea or breakfast and can be had in most hotels and restaurants around. Close by: Station and Imperial. Also some useful shops. (Main St. half a mile). Tourist info, café and some visitor attractions down at the harbour, with interesting museum nearby.

The Abbey, founded 1178, was resting place (1951) for Stone of Destiny after its 'removal' from Westminster Abbey.

Railwayana
Opened Dundee & Arbroath Railway October 6 1838, originally the terminus of that line. Rebuilt Caledonian & N.B. with two platforms 1911. Plain, solid school-style with a steel roof and cast iron columns, typical of the turn of the century.

A fine mural panel on Platform 1, *(see left)* signed by Charles Anderson, RSW, records 'The Signing of the Declaration of Arbroath, April 6 1320'.

As it leaves Arbroath en route to Dundee the line runs briefly alongside the tracks of Kerr's Miniature Railway. A plaque, also on Platform 1, remembers 'Matthew B Kerr (1943-2006), proprietor of Scotland's Oldest Miniature Railway.'

Distances
Glasgow, Queen Street 100 miles; Edinburgh, Waverley 76 miles; Aberdeen 54 miles; Dundee 17 miles.

ARDGAY
IV24 3AQ (Highland)

Guidelines
Until May 1977 this was known as Bonar Bridge, but the name change was only sensible since that's where the station is. Station house morphed into a b & b and just next door was a general store of the type that sold everything – including the Sunday papers – they once arrived off a newspaper special which ran all the way north from London.

Though the general store (and the large road house opposite) have long since closed their doors, an enterprising country supplies store, complete with café, grew from a former filling station nearby. Bonar Bridge, a mile or so away, has facilities a'plenty, for long boasting a well stocked art materials store too.

Railwayana
Opened October 1 1864 by HR, remarkably well preserved original buildings with typical pre-1870 columns supporting small awning.

Ardgay marks start of Highland Line's first serious meander into the country, one of several caused either by geography and/or the vagaries of Highland lairds. In this case it was the need to skirt the Kyle of Sutherland and travel up river to a suitable crossing point at Invershin, all of which could have been remedied in later years had rail and road shared the new Meikle Ferry crossing.

Distances
Inverness 56 miles, Wick 104 miles, Thurso 96 miles

Viewed from the line
Going south, Highland malt distilleries at Balblair and, near Tain, Glemmorangie.

ARDLUI
G83 8SW (Argyll & Bute)

Guidelines
Spectacularly situated at northern end of Loch Lomond, on the fringes of the Loch Lomond and the Trossachs National Park. Though little more than a scattering of cottages, visitors are well catered for. Short walk from the station, Ardlui Hotel, holiday home park and shop, plus campsite and marina. West Highland Way, which runs along opposite shore of the loch, can be accessed by on-demand seasonally run ferry operated by the Hotel.

Railwayana
Opened August 1894, Ardlui is an island platform station with subway access. Main station building demolished in 1970 due to 'subsidence', but the signal cabin survives as a waiting room. In 'Sprinter' times, Ardlui has been principal passing place for north and southbound services. Sidings, occasionally used by engineers, rusting reminder of the days of the pick up goods train.

Distances
Glasgow Queen Street 51 miles; Oban 50; Fort William 71; Mallaig 113.

Most Westerly
Station In
Britain

ARISAIG
PH39 4NJ (Highland)

Guidelines
Thanks to *mv Shearwater,* Arisaig became popular as an alternative to Mallaig as a starting point for crossings to the Small Isles – principally Eigg and Muck. Some of the summer sailings connect with train arrivals, but be sure to check in advance, as nothing is for ever.

Railwayana
Opened by the West Highland April 1 1901. This two platform station with, reputedly, haunted waiting rooms, proclaims itself the 'Most Westerly' in Britain.

A plaque on Platform 1 marks the 2009 'refurbishment' of the station, funded by the Railway Heritage Trust, the Highland Rail Partnership and Hitrans.

When steam returned to the line in the summer of 1984 Arisaig was the farthest point reached by the venerable Maude *(see left)* under her own power – and that was quite a struggle.

Distances
Glasgow Queen Street 157 miles; Mallaig 7 miles; Fort William 34 miles.

Once a private halt for nearby Attadale House, now mainly useful for the annual Highland Games held there, or for garden visits.

Across the water could once be seen the ghost village of smart wooden houses built for execs. for the short lived Kishorn oil platform construction yard.

Railwayana
Opened by Dingwall and Skye Railway on August 10 1870. Original simple but charming buildings replaced by the usual brutalist concrete block job.

Attadale had originally been earmarked as the first terminus for the Kyle Line. Grandiose plans prepared by Alexander Ross, an Inverness architect, included refreshment and waiting rooms and a smart hotel towering above all else.

Internal squabbles and money problems prevented any of this ever being built and the railway eventually pushed on another four or five miles to Strome where a miserable wooden platform and pier were built.

Closed to goods August 15 1966. Freight siding and ground frame *(seen in picture below)* removed 1979.

Distances
Inverness 67 miles; Kyle of Lochalsh 15 miles.

Aviemore

Until the 60s Aviemore was just another Victorian Highland resort with stone villas dotted around in close proximity to the railway station. Then along came the Aviemore Centre.

Cruelly referred to by some as the biggest motorway service area in Britain, the centre does in fact offer a wide range of facilities to kids and their long-suffering parents (at a price!) Skating rinks, swimming pools, a real live cinema, dry ski slope, karting, shopping centre and even once, a Santa Claus Land!

All this commercial development has attracted other initiatives, like the Dalfaber time-sharing holiday village, complete with sporting complex, including what could well be the most northerly indoor tennis court in the UK – (or not).

Further retail adventurism has led to the opening of a new shopping centre bang next door to the station itself. Fast food, pizzas, chip shop, even a bookshop.

Railwayana

Opened by Inverness & Perth Junction Railway September 9 1863 and dramatically enlarged and remodelled by Highland Railway 1892. Four platforms, footbridge and waiting rooms on both islands.

The preserved Strathspey Railway has its own platform *(shown bottom left)*, whence trains steam to Boat of Garten *(q.v.)* during summer months and some holiday weekends. Station's original four-track stone engine shed dates from 1863.

In 1910, at the height of Scotland's railway mania, the Strathpeffer Spa Express left Aviemore every Tuesday for the Spa, with just one stop at Dingwall, by-passing even Inverness on its way!

Distances

Inverness 34 miles; Perth 83 miles; Glasgow, Queen Street 146 miles; Edinburgh, Waverley 156 miles; London, Euston 533 miles.

AYR
KA7 3AU (Ayrshire)

Guidelines
Ayr is for Burns buffs. Tam o'Shanter Burns Museum in the High Street and Land o'Burns centre in Alloway. Also on hand two miles of sandy beach, Ayr racecourse, golf courses everywhere and occasional visits from the paddle steamer Waverley. Gaiety Theatre is the home of nudge, nudge/wink, wink variety, once starring Rikki Fulton, Jimmy Logan and other stalwarts of the Scottish stage.

For many a year a branch line ran to Butlin's holiday camp south of the city near Doonfoot.

Railwayana
Original station opened by Glasgow, Paisley, Kilmarnock & Ayr Railway July 15 1837. Rebuilt by Glasgow & South Western Railway 1886. Dominated by imposing Franco-American mansardic-style hotel *(seen left)*, sold by BR as early as 1951! Design: Andrew Galloway, engineer to G & SW Railway; cost: £50,000. Now a B listed building.

Note the floridly ornate cast iron roof trusses in train shed.

Distances
Glasgow, Central 40.5 miles; Stranraer 59 miles.

BALLOCH ('CENTRAL')
G83 8SS (West Dunbartonshire)

Guidelines
When *The Maid of the Loch* plied every summer on Loch Lomond the 'Central' (introduced June 30 1952) was needed to distinguish this from Balloch Pier *(seen left);* when both were closed, the replacement station over the road became plain Balloch once more when it opened in 1988. The handsome old station took on a new lease of life as the local tourist information centre (complete with a natty modern portaloo just outside).

Just north east of station and over the bridge is departure point for water borne tours round the loch.

Railwayana
Opened by Edinburgh & Glasgow Railway July 15 1850, the two-platform complex, including imposing early Victorian stationmaster's house with incongruous 'greenhouse' stuck on the front, was closed in 1988 to be replaced, across the road, by a couple of orange modular boxes from BR's lego kit. The move did dispense with the need for a level crossing.

Distances
Glasgow, Queen St. 19 miles via Clydebank; 21 miles via Singer.

PH33 7JF (Highland)

Guidelines
Banavie was built as a short extension to the West Highland railway shortly after it reached Fort William in 1894. The idea was to link up with pleasure boats using Telford's Caledonian Canal. Today that is just about the only reason you would get off here. A small hotel overlooks the sequence of eight locks known as Neptune's Staircase. Good vantage point to view Ben Nevis — if it's free of cloud.

Railwayana
Original Banavie station, now a private house, opened June 1895. It became Banavie Pier when the Mallaig line opened in 1901. A new station *(below)* opened then at Banavie Junction. This was duly demolished following BR (shortsighted) policy and replaced by the usual jaunty bus shelter. This notwithstanding the fact that BR themselves had up to that moment been using in their publicity a most attractive colour shot of the old station lit up against the snow!

      Massive steel swing bridge over the Caledonian Canal *(see left)* designed by Simpson & Wilson in 1901 and still in daily use. Banavie branch line to the pier closed September 2 1939.

Distances
Glasgow, Queen Street 125 miles; Mallaig 39 miles; Fort William 2 miles.

BERWICK-UPON-TWEED
TD15 1NF (Northumberland)

Guidelines
Berwick is not strictly within the scope of this publication, but merits a mention if only for the 'revenge' taken by the North British Railway when they first established a station here in 1844. In 1482 Berwick and its castle had "finally surrendered to England" (as *Encyclopedia Britannica* put it). The NB hit back in 1844, destroying most of what remained of the castle and using the stone in their castellated station and train sheds.

Present station built by the London and North Eastern in 1927 in red Dumfriess-shire sandstone. The name was displayed in art nouveau lettering.

Also in Berwick: Royal Border Bridge, designed by Robert Stephenson and T.E. Harrison, built on foundation of American elm driven in to the river bed by a Nasmyth hammer. Opened September 1850 by Queen Victoria.

Distances
Edinburgh, Waverley 57 miles; Dunbar 28 miles; London, King's Cross 336 miles

BLAIR ATHOLL
PH18 5SL (Highland)

Guidelines
Handy for village of Blair Atholl, a quieter and more pleasant place once by-passed by the A9. Hotels, craft shop and an excellent caravan and camping site in grounds of Blair Castle, home since 1269 to the Duke of Atholl. Grounds and part of castle open to public during summer; tearoom and shop. HQ of Atholl Highlanders, only officially recognised private army in Great Britain, so beware!

Railwayana
Opened by Inverness & Perth Junction Railway, September 9 1863. Until LMS days very much the Duke's own station. New buildings (subsequently altered) completed July 1869 to designs approved by His Grace. For many years he was entitled, literally, to red carpet treatment when his train arrived. Closed to goods November 7 1966. (Official change of spelling – from Blair Athole – September 7 1893).

Distances
Inverness 83 miles; Perth 35 miles; Glasgow, Queen St. 98 miles; Edinburgh, Waverley 108 miles; London Euston 485 miles.

Viewed from the line
The Tilt Viaduct built 1863 by Joseph Mitchell. A lattice truss bridge with castellated arches.

BOAT OF GARTEN
PH24 3BH (Highland)

Guidelines
Only fully fledged standard gauge privately operated station in Scotland, part of the Strathspey Steam Railway. Excellent railway shop, refreshments and Boat Hotel hard by for drinks, meals etc. Over the road PO, shops etc.

Station is open daily during the summer season and weekends during the off-season. Details of steam operations from Aviemore station, tourist information offices or *www.strathspeysteamrailway.co.uk*

Railwayana
Opened Inverness and Perth Junction Railway August 3 1863. Closed to passengers October 18 1965 and fully closed June 16 1969.

Line (together with Aviemore engine shed) bought by the Strathspey Railway Company in 1972 for the sum of £44,250.

After a couple of specials run for benefit of railways' directors and friends, line re-opened to the public after much toil and not a little tribulation July 22 1978. Steady progress has since been made to drive the line to Grantown once more.

Class 5 No 5025, built in 1934, is amongst the railway's proud possessions and has been known to travel as far as Kyle of Lochalsh!

Distances
Aviemore 5 miles; Broomhill *(aka Glenbogle)* 5 miles

From here rail and road part company as the tracks cross the wilderness of Rannoch Moor. B. of O. itself is really no more than an hotel (and bunkhouse). Both station and hotel are right on the route of the West Highland Way (it uses the station underpass) so the hotel is used to catering for hungry and thirsty travellers.

For a while the station buildings catered for walkers as the West Highland Sleeper, but problems with water supplies proved an obstacle.

Railwayana
Opened by West Highland Railway August 3 1894. Standard island platform vintage building with dark green doors, light green shingle-faced walls and mass concrete platforms. Clock by James Ritchie & Son, Edinburgh, no longer in business!

Distances
Glasgow, Queen St. 72 miles; Mallaig 93 miles; Ft.Wm. 51 miles

Viewed from the line
Some three miles to the north the ruins of Achallader Castle where, legend has it, the Campbells planned the massacre of Glencoe. A few miles farther on is Gorton, a passing loop where once a private station ran, for a while, a school for local rail children in a carriage on the platform.

Not all attempts to bring industry to Brora have been successful. The coal mine closed and at least one local distillery has gone the same way. A textile business flourished for a while, latterly occupying very ambitious premises on the outskirts of town but though the name lived on, the local connection was lost.

Handy for the station, shops and a little farther away hotels and b & bs and, believe it or not, a sandy beach, bordered by famous golf links.

These were some of the lands to which the hapless Highlanders were herded during the Clearances. Kintradwell Brock, some two and a half miles N. of Brora, is a ninth century fortified tower.

Railwayana
Opened by Highland Railway June 19, 1871, rebuilt 1895 in a solid no-nonsense Board school style with terracotta ridge tiles. Only windows and finials facing the main platform are ornamentally treated. Handsome timber goods building *(shown left)* survived longer than many of its contemporaries.

Distances
Inverness 90 miles; Wick 71 miles; Thurso 63 miles.

Broughty Ferry

Originally built to serve the jute barons of Dundee, Broughty Ferry has become one more suburb of the city. Known today more for yachting and sail-boarding than for jute JRs! Fifteenth century B. Castle has been turned into a museum telling the story of Dundee's whaling past.

Broughty harbour laid out by rail engineer T. Grainger.

Railwayana

Opened by Dundee & Arbroath Railway October 6 1838. Original structure much added to and altered. The elaborate outback bridge linking the two platforms (*pictured*) did not survive the modernisers. The sturdy crossing gates too went, to be replaced by the usual combination of flashing lights – and cameras.

For some time the station was without any form of sign, presumably an attempt to fool any invading force, but the mid-80's bout of self-promotion by Scotrail led to the putting in place of the standard issue sans serif signs and a tasteful paint job.

Distances

Dundee 4 miles; Aberdeen 67 miles; Edinburgh, Waverley 63 miles.

Guidelines

Agricola got here a year or two before the railway did — more than a thousand years earlier, in fact. He built a fortalice on Dunearn Hill. In the 12th century, the Abbots of Dunfermline got Rossend Castle together. Mary Q. of S. stayed here and then the place fell into a ruinous state until bought in the 70s by an Edinburgh firm of architects who went about the task of restoring it.

The harbour and once busy shipyards have managed to hold on to some oil-related fabrication activity, though an alumina plant in the dock area did not survive long into the present century.

Railwayana

Original station opened September 17 1847 by Edinburgh, Perth & Dundee Railway, but its imposing neo-classical buildings *(below and left)* remained sadly unused and neglected until eventually given a new lease of life as a business centre.

Today's two platforms, served by economy NB railway brick and wood structure, were opened on completion of Forth Bridge. Original station's architect is unknown, but stone capitals are of similar style to those on façade of the long demolished Edinburgh Canal Street Station – on the site of the Waverley Market, just next to the NB Hotel.

Distances

Edinburgh, Waverley 20 miles; Arbroath 56 miles.

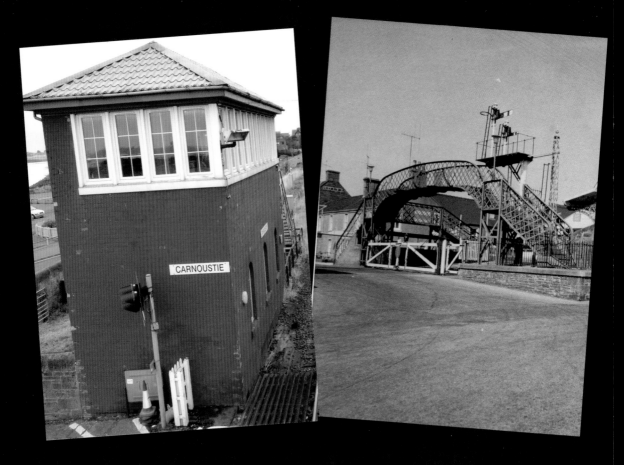

CARNOUSTIE
DD7 6AY (Angus)

Guidelines
Not quite such a choice of courses as St Andrews, but since they closed the branch from Leuchars, far more accessible to the golfing rail traveller. Hotels a-plenty all around, but don't expect to get in to them when The Open hits town!

Public phone on the road near the station and most facilities in town.

Railwayana
Opened by the Dundee & Arbroath Railway October 6 1838. Original small stone building has become a private house (note the unusual chevroned gables). The replacement station, a two-platform affair with attractive wooden buildings, was put up by the D & A at the turn of the century. Very late example of a canopy resting on highly ornate cast iron cantilevers *(see below)*, sadly demolished in 1986 and replaced by variations on the ubiquitous bus shelter.

In a rare access of enthusiasm in the early 60s, the purpose-built Golf Street platform was opened specially for golfers, but very few trains stop there.

Distances
Dundee 10 miles; Aberdeen 60 miles; Edinburgh, Waverley 70 miles.

CARRBRIDGE (or CARR BRIDGE)
PH23 3AJ (Highland)

Guidelines
Slightly removed from metropolis of Carrbridge itself, but it's worth a visit nonetheless, especially if you trek out to the enterprising Landmark visitor centre — one of the earliest such centres to be established in the north. Audio-visual display, bookshop, sculpture park + restaurant/snack bar. Also in CB: hotels, shops, golf course.

Opposite the station, and possibly a wee bit optimistically, is a mighty industrial estate, with space for expansion.

Railwayana
Opened 1892 by the Highland Railway. One of the finest wooden stations developed by the HR. Another, less easily seen, is at Plockton on the Kyle line. The centre space between the two gable ends of the main building is covered by a slated awning supported by cast iron columns. At the north end is an attached signal office, attractively glazed.

In 1914 disaster struck when the wooden bridge over the nearby Baddengorm Burn collapsed under a passing train with appalling consequences, killing five passengers

Distances
Inverness 28 miles; Aviemore 8 miles.

CARSTAIRS
ML11 8PR (South Lanarkshire)

Guidelines
Carstairs is known as a railway village (at one stage the Caledonian had its own school there) but there is a village of the same name nearby with a pleasant village green. But looming over everything is the grim 'State Hospital' (as this penal institution is euphemistically called) with its high metal fence cutting into the skyline.

Station itself once boasted a wide range of facilities for travellers changing trains but today it's a super bus shelter with phone and loos, still partially staffed.

Many London bound fliers whistle through without so much as a thought for the past, and what a speed they can go!

Railwayana
Carstairs Junction came into being when the Caledonian Railway linked up its Edinburgh and Glasgow services to its line south to Carlisle in the mid 1840s. The first station here opened on February 15 1848. The two-platform island station was rebuilt 1913-14 with noteworthy mild steel cantilevers supporting the roof canopy. Look out for the interesting wrought iron truss bridge just S. of Carstairs.

Distances
Glasgow, Central 29 miles; Edinburgh, Wav. 28 miles; London, Euston 373 miles.

CORPACH
PH33 7LS (Highland)

Guidelines
With the coming of the Scottish Pulp and Paper Mill it seemed the future of Corpach would be a bright one, but by 1980 the pulp mill side had been forced to close and Corpach's golden age seemed over. The paper mill continued for a while but eventually gave way for what has been described as Europe's biggest sawmill.

Some development where the canal terminates – the Caledonian Canal meets the sea here – could prove more successful.

Out on the road a handy Co-op, hotels and 'Road to the Isles' type b & bs, as well as rare rocks museum.

Railwayana
Opened by the West Highland April 1 1901. The quaint pre-war wooden structure *(see left)* retained its own stationmaster for many years, but a private house eventually displaced this humble structure and the 'station' function was taken over by a bus shelter. Private sidings served the mill nearby, with a regular timber shuttle from Crianlarich bringing business for a while.

Distances
Fort William 4 miles; Mallaig 38 miles; Glasgow, Q. St. 127 miles.

Corrour

CORROUR
PH30 4AA (Highland)

Guidelines
To get off here it is advisable to plan ahead: Corrour is the station and nothing else, though there is a youth hostel a mile or so away on L. Ossian. Only fairly recently has the station been accessible at all by track; rail staff and their needs still tend to travel by train.

All around is the bleak vastness of Rannoch Moor, notorious for its bogs and peat hags. Mists descend without warning and in the featureless and awe-inspiring landscape many a life has been lost – so beware!

From the security of the carriage, however, look out for the rare sight of the herds of red deer grazing and golden eagles soaring.

Railwayana
Corrour was built as a passing place and for the first years of its existence was effectively a private station.

On September 15 1934, it was formally declared open to the public!
On March 1 1965 it was 'closed to goods', so any bales of hay that had to be transported had to go in the guard's van – where such existed. *(See picture left).*

Welcome visitor facilities provided by local estate, whose lodge at the far end of Loch Laidon was replaced by the structure shown top right on facing page.

Distances
Fort William 28 miles; Glasgow, Queen Street 95 miles; Mallaig 70 miles.

Crianlarich

CRIANLARICH
FK20 8QN (Stirlingshire)

Guidelines
Until you reach it Crianlarich seems as though it might turn out to be the centre of the universe. To the driver all roads in west cemtral Scotland seem to lead there and in the days of the old Callander & Oban railway it was something of a railway Mecca too. Station tearoom has had its ups and downs, so always wise to plan ahead. No more breakfast baskets, alas, as in the good old days, but still a well earned reputation for decent refreshments and some home baking.

Crianlarich itself has a couple of pubs, a hotel and plenty of b & b's along with PO/stores and a smart new youth hostel just beside the station. A spur leads off the West Highland Way, the long distance footpath that links Glasgow and Fort William.

Railwayana
When it opened in August 1894, Crianlarich was a handy half-way house on the West Highland route to Fort William. It was also the ideal spot for an interchange between the West Highland and the Callander & Oban. A scheme was agreed and the work was completed in October 1894, but it was fully three years before the two companies could agree on how to work the link and the junction did not open until December of 1897.

Crianlarich continued to perform a vital role in servicing men and machines right until the steam era ended. The introduction of dining cars in the late 20's sadly curtailed the catering services offered by the Crianlarich dining room — at one stage breakfast, luncheon, tea and dinner baskets were available. But two chance events in the sixties had far-reaching effects.

The first was a fire in March 1962 which destroyed the main station buildings, while three years later, on the night of September 27 1965, the Crianlarich to Callander line was blocked by a landslide in Glen Ogle.*

When steam disappeared there was no longer the need for the enormous quantities of water once required at Crianlarich and the water towers which dominated the station were demolished.

Against all the odds the fine brick built train shed has survived and in recent years some of the railway houses near the station have been refurbished. There is life in the system yet! How about a Highland outdoor railway museum to celebrate the fact?

Distances
Glasgow, Queen St. 60 miles; Mallaig 105 miles; Ft. William 63 miles; Oban 42 miles.

* An event graphically remembered in a poem in the pages of Steam Lines, a collection of railway verses.

CULRAIN
IV27 4ET (Highland)

Guidelines
This once was where to get off if you felt like living it up on your YH card by
staying at nearby Carbisdale Castle, an enormous grey whinstone pile *(top left)*
completed in 1914. Alas, you can hostel it no more. The property was sold off to
the highest bidder and has reverted to private ownership. (It was built originally
for the estranged Duchess of Sutherland, who, it is rumoured, gazed down
contemptuously as the Duke trundled past in his private train on the bridge across
the River Oykel, below.)

Railwayana
Opened July 1 1870 by the Sutherland Railway. Original building removed. Small
wooden shelter and single platform now look as though they serve a field not a
railway. Closed to goods (bags of manure?) May 18 1964.

Distances
Inverness 61 miles; Wick 100 miles; Thurso 93 miles.

Viewed from the line
(Travelling north) Oykel Viaduct, a B listed wrought-iron lattice girder bridge over
the river Oykel and on the left, Carbisdale Castle.

Guidelines

Cupar is home to a number of enterprising businesses whose products cover the country. The bakery, patisserie and chocolaterie brand Fisher and Donaldson are headquartered here, as are the famous Fife outdoor clothing and footwear firm Hoggs of Fife. In easy walking distance of the station a branch of the upwardly mobile 'discounter' Lidl.

At nearby Ceres, a charming round-the-green village with its own highland games as well as the Fife Folk Museum. Also close by the Kingarrock traditional hickory golf course at Hill of Tarvit.

Railwayana

Opened by Edinburgh, Perth & Dundee Railway, September 17 1847. Both station and adjoining road bridge are B listed and The Railway Heritage of Britain called it 'perhaps the most important surviving early railway station in Scotland in terms of architectural distinction and completeness'. Architect unknown, but thought to be David Bell.

Some rather unfortunate sixties face-lifting at the entrance, but signs of affection in platform planting (in tractor tyres) and hanging baskets of geraniums.

To the north of the station stood an enormous four storey sandstone goods warehouse built over arches *(shown left, before its demolition)*.

Distances

Edinburgh, Waverley 45 miles; Dundee 15 miles; London, King's X 438 miles

Dalmally once advertised its presence to the passing motorist with a combined village sign offering craft shop, hotel, PO and b & b. The train lands you right bang in the middle of the village and all are (or were once!) within walking distance.

Down the road is the Cruachan power scheme, a spectacular pumped storage power station hidden away in the middle of a mountain. Visits throughout the summer. The re-opening of Loch Awe station made access a whole lot easier.

Dalmally Mart and Show are agricultural high points of the summer. Tin tabernacle hall *(shown left)* one of the finest, if distressed, examples of corrugated iron architecture in the Highlands.

Railwayana
Opened C & O May 1 1877 and for a while terminus of the line while they struggled to raise the money to drive on to the Atlantic at Oban. Apart from an elegant station, the only sign of this earlier role is a long-disused siding.

Elegant glazed, pitched awning on iron columns *(see below)* has managed to survive for many a year – but for how much longer?

Note variety of stone and brick used in station building and nearby bridge.

Distances
Glasgow, Queen Street 77 miles; Oban 25 miles

DALMENY
EH30 9JU (City of Edinburgh)

Guidelines
Overshadowed by the Forth Bridge – almost literally – best excuse for getting off here would be to catch a distant glimpse of that masterpiece. But Dalmeny itself, slightly south of the station, has its attractions. Known mainly for its Rosebery connections, it boasts a village green and a 12th century church restored in the 30s.

The oil age gave Dalmeny a new dimension with the commissioning of the tanker terminal at Hound Point. Oil is piped down from Aberdeen to be loaded on to supertankers in the Forth.

Railwayana
Opened by the NB June 2 1890 to serve Forth Bridge traffic. The attractive wooden building had survived relatively unscathed, lit by gas. In 1978 electricity was installed for the first time and, coincidence or not, the building was gutted by fire on November 29 1980. While bridge itself is A listed, Dalmeny station buildings themselves are B. Also to be seen: former Forth Bridge Railway Company office building lying disused.

Distances
Edinburgh, Waverley 10 miles; Kirkcaldy 17 miles.

Another of the backwaters created by the new A9, Dalwhinnie has still quite a lot to offer the visitor who makes the effort to stop here. A good hotel, one of the last remaining transport cafés on the whole road, b & b and a surviving garage, not to mention a shoppie too. There is also a distillery a mile or so from the station *(see picture left),* owned by Diageo and usually open for visits (wise to check, though).

When the skiing grounds above Aviemore are crowded out, Dalwhinnie could be a crafty place to lay your head.

Railwayana
Opened by Inverness & Perth Junction, September 9 1863. Contractors for the original buildings and permanent way were Gowans & Mackay. Two platforms and a footbridge. A plaque erected by Scotrail in 2004 records how: "General Montgomery stayed in Dalwhinnie in his special train Rapier for a four day rest period during his planning of the D-Day landings."

This notwithstanding, Dalwhinnie was closed to goods on February 26 1967!

Distances
Inverness 60 miles; Perth 59 miles; London, Euston 509 miles

Dingwall

THIS RAILWAY STATION WAS USED AS A
TEA STALL FOR SAILORS AND SOLDIERS FROM
20TH SEPTEMBER 1915. UNTIL 12TH APRIL 1919
IN CONNECTION WITH THE ROSS AND CROMARTY
COUNTY BRANCH RED CROSS SOCIETY.
DURING WHICH PERIOD 134.864 MEN WERE
SUPPLIED WITH TEA.

Guidelines

Successive by-passes and new roads have taken more and more traffic away from the heart of Dingwall. Station occupies a pretty central position, within easy reach of shops, hotels and cafés. Lively hostelry on platform itself. Both bus and taxi operators have also set up within the confines of the station.

After many years of brave struggle the station bookstall, first a John Menzies effort and latterly run by a succession of private entrepreneurs, finally pulled down the shutters.

Railwayana

Opened by the Inverness & Ross-shire Railway June 11 1862 and rebuilt by the Highland 1886. Fine awning, similar to that at (closed) Strathpeffer Spa.

As late as the 1950s there were still more than 100 employees at Dingwall, many charged with looking after the cattle pens, which still survive.

A plaque records the serving during the war of an inordinate number of cups of tea to servicemen passing through. Today in the station itself a cuppa could be harder to come by.

Dingwall is the starting point for very wonderful Skye railway to Kyle.

Distances

Inverness 19 miles; Kyle of Lochalsh 64 miles; Wick 143 miles; Thurso 135 miles

Guidelines

Having (just) survived the Beeching axe in the 60s (along with North Berwick and Longniddry) and lived through a period when buses seemed set to take over local services, Drem was born again with the development of the North Berwick branch and its eventual electrification. With the redevelopment of the old goods yard as station car park it became a popular commuter station for Edinburgh-bound workers, with substantial numbers using it annually.

Railwayana

Opened NB Railway 1846. North Berwick branch opened three years later. At one stage this line was horse driven in an attempt to save money. The carriage used for this pioneering service can be seen on display in the York National Railway Museum.

Two platforms, main station buildings now private house. Goods yard survived until 1979 and was then re-developed as station car park.

In the 80s A BR destruction team set about eliminating the station buildings, starting with the (listed) waiting room opposite main station building. Loud protests led to them being forced to restore the structure to its original design (see picture left).

Distances

Edinburgh Waverley 18 miles; North Berwick 5 miles

DUMBARTON CENTRAL
G82 1PZ (West Dunbartonshire)

Guidelines
A road scheme slicing through the middle of the town left Dumbarton's main station somewhat isolated from its high street, but the planners did graciously concede an underpass so you could struggle through to the rebuilt town square. Nearer the station the scene is somewhat desolate, though look out for the sandstone municipal buildings which once sported the red flag (Dumbarton has been twinned with Nicaragua).

Railwayana
The present station — it became 'Central' on March 3 1952 — was a rebuild job begun in 1896 and opened October 4 1898 by the Dumbarton & Balloch Joint Line Committee. They did a good job, but sadly BR and its successors have not been able to do their work much justice. The original two-island, four platform layout, reached up finely decorated stairs from street level, has seen one platform closed off completely. Weathered sandstone capitals *(top left)* recall a grander past.

Gothic style mild steel awning reflects Caley rather than NB influence.

Neighbouring Dumbarton East fell victim to a BR hit squad, though similar in style, it was unceremoniously razed to the ground in 1984, though, to be fair, some attempt was made to retain the street entrance.

Distances
Glasgow, Queen Street 15 miles via Clydebank; 16 miles via Singer; Fort William 107 miles; Mallaig 149 miles.

Dumfries

DUMFRIES
DG1 1NF (Dumfries & Galloway)

Guidelines
Despite its very reduced role as a rail hub – once it was the junction for a whole series of branch lines – Dumfries station is anything but dead. And it's not afraid to proclaim the fact. Wall plaques record the winning in 1987 of the Best Station Award (mainly thanks to the efforts of rail worker Jack Aitken) while imaginative planting and landscaping around the station buildings won a final place in a recent Best Station Garden contest.

The elegant former station bookstall discreetly advertises an informal collection of rail memorabilia under the banner of Railway Reflections, while another former station building has become a River of Life church. A factory complex accessed from the station's former goods yard was for many years famous for the production of Carnation milk and its cousin CoffeeMate, but time took its toll and the site was subsequently re-developed as an industrial estate.

Railwayana
Opened by the Glasgow, Dumfries & Carlisle Railway sometime in 1848. Original four platforms linked by an elaborate wood and iron covered footbridge, possibly of 1880s vintage. Much of the present sandstone building is known to have been in existence in 1868, but is thought to have been drastically remodelled. A glazed awning seems a late 19th century addition. B listed.

Distances
Glasgow, Central 82 miles; Carlisle 33 miles; London, Euston 332 miles.

Guidelines
Dunbar Castle has seen plenty of action in its time. Mary Q of S stayed (twice) and it was defended under siege by the formidable Black Agnes back in C14.

Innumerable hotels and guest houses and a lot of golf gets played. Belhaven beer is put into those familiar bottles and nearby is Torness nuclear power station, which no one now seems to need. Cockburnspath to the S. is the starting point for the Southern Upland Way which runs cross-country to the Irish Sea.

Railwayana
Opened June 22 1846 by the NB. Built on a curve in the local red sandstone and heavily altered this century, but still incorporating 1846 structure. Track layout remodelled 1974 and in 1976 both East and West signal boxes closed and the line came under control of Edinburgh Signalling Centre. For many years after privatisation Dunbar remained part of the East Coast franchise *(see GNER livery in pic below)* before coming under Scotrail stewardship.

An *Illustrated London News* from 1858 recorded that on, September 7, 'a monster train of excursionists' stopped at Dunbar to welcome the Royal train on its journey northward.

Distances
Edinburgh, Waverley 29 miles; Newcastle 95 miles; London, King's X 364 miles.

Guidelines

If you wanted to learn about catering and hotel management this was once the stop for you. Originally the home of Sir Alexander Matheson, one of the great Highland Railway builders, Duncraig Castle *(seen left from the air)* was latterly turned over for a while to further education for domestic science, catering, etc.

A fine view from the station across the bay to Plockton and there's a route to walk there, but it's probably easier to get off at Plockton station itself *(q.v.)*.

Railwayana

Opened as 'Duncraig Platform' November 2 1897 by HR as a private station — which it remained until May 23 1949. On September 10 1962 the 'Platform' part was dropped. On December 7 1964 the station was officially closed. But the buildings were mysteriously maintained and, such are still the ways of the Highlands, trains continued to call. In December 1975, Duncraig returned to the timetables and was given a new lease of life.

The charming octagonal summer house on the platform is the original waiting room and has been beautifully painted in the traditional steam era chocolate and white livery. The enterprising Scottish Chamber Orchestra once performed here in the open on a Highland summer tour.

Distances

Inverness 76 miles; Kyle of Lochalsh 7 miles.

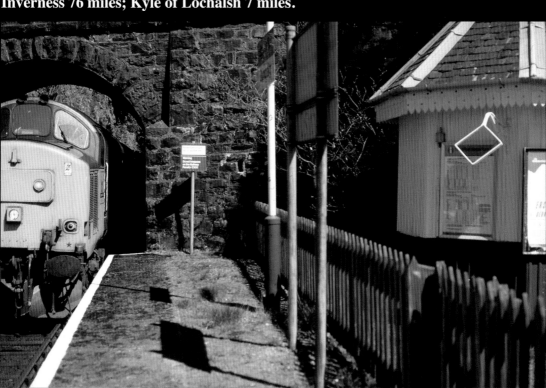

Dundee

or a short part of its way, the line through Dundee becomes a Metro – trouble is there is today just one stop. Dundee's 'underground' does however put that station at the centre of the new Waterfront development, bang opposite the new outpost of the V & A museum, a showcase building designed to 'do a Bilbao' for the city of jam, jute and journalism. Gone is the 'mirror' facade shown reflecting the changing city in the upper picture opposite.

In its place a multi storey, budget priced hotel of some 120 rooms due to open its doors in time for the opening of the V & A. *(Artist's impression below.)*

Railwayana
Opened by NB May 31 1878. Interesting original wrought-iron roof on columns with very bold Gothic brackets, built by Wright, Young & Company and designed by Charles S Johnston, a pupil of that great baronial architect David Bryce.

'New' booking hall and façade opened February 2 1959, refreshment room modernised 1974. Then re-located during eighties refurbishment, with the introduction of a Quicksnack counter bringing fast food to the banks of the silvery Tay. During the latest major re-modelling of the station a (modest) temporary entrance was created on Riverside Drive in the midst of the oft-re-organised inner ring road system.

Distances
Edinburgh, Wav. 60 miles; Glasgow, Queen St. 83 miles; Aberdeen 71 miles; Perth 22m

Viewed from the line
The second — and successful — Tay Bridge which opened June 20 1887, at 2 miles 364 yards the longest railway bridge in Britain. One or two truncated stone piers of the old bridge still appear above the waves. Designer Thomas Bouch had to abandon work on a possible follow-up on the Forth.

Top right: a voice from a BR past – 'No facilities' at this station – still, alas, true.

DUNKELD & BIRNAM
PH8 0DP (Perth & Kinross)

Guidelines
The 'new' A9 came between Dunkeld (and Birnam) and its railway station, but to be fair, the station was never particularly handy for Dunkeld, being on the other side of the Tay. A pedestrian underpass at the north end of the station leads under the road to Dunkeld, with a branch immediately off to the right which leads down to Birnam – main attraction the cleverly restored and developed Birnam Institute arts centre (which boasts a Beatrix Potter wing) – well worth a visit – *(see picture)*.

Besides a number of hotels and a Co-op, Dunkeld boasts an excellent deli, a small gallery, tourist info and a busy National Trust for Scotland shop.

Railwayana
Opened April 7 1856 by Perth & Dunkeld Railway. Two platforms linked by a fine Victorian iron footbridge. Gas lighting continued to be used for many years and there is still a lamp post thought to date from the 1860s.

Station building a magnificent example of recreated Tudor, designed by Andrew Heiton of Perth. Described by one authority as 'of magnificence unique in Scotland', this B listed gem has been all but abandoned and is, of course, unstaffed *(see sign left)*. An early attempt by local interests to create a small railway museum in the building met, sadly, with little enthusiasm.

Distances
Inverness 103 miles; Perth 16 miles; London, Euston 465 miles.

Viewed from the line (going North)
If you're smart about it – decorated road bridge and tunnel entrance at The Hermitage, just north of Dunkeld.

DUNROBIN CASTLE
KW10 6SF (Highland)

Guidelines
Dunrobin was very much the private station for the Duke of Sutherland and Dunrobin Castle, standing as it does in the trees just opposite the main entrance to the castle. In a commendable display of enterprise BR undertook in 1985 the reopening, at least during the summer months, of the charming 'summer house' station for visitors to the castle.

Castle and extensive grounds, together with shop and teashop, are open throughout the summer, an earlier attempt to create a Gordonstoun-type bare knees and cold showers boys' school having foundered in the 60s. An exclusive Swiss form of time-share operation was then mooted as a replacement.

Railwayana
Opened in 1870 by the Duke of Sutherland's Railway to serve his own line from Golspie to West Helmsdale and rebuilt in 1902. For a while the Duke's line operated a twice-daily service between the two points until it was eventually absorbed into the Highland Railway, when it drove right through to the far north.

Ornate waiting room is Category B listed.

Distances
Inverness 86 miles; Wick 76 miles.

EDINBURGH WAVERLEY
EH1 1BB

Guidelines

Edinburgh Waverley itself would almost justify its own guidebook. For the purposes of this guide we shall limit ourselves to the actual block in which the station finds itself.

The whole site is dominated by the North British Hotel built for the Company in 1902 after the most exhaustive research — a special sub-committee toured Europe to get ideas. As part of the privatisation mania that has gripped the country, BR were ordered to sell all their station hotels. Scotland's finest three, Gleneagles, the NB and the 'Caley' at the other end of Princes Street were sold off ahead of the others.

Next door to the hotel, the old Waverley market, occupying the top corner of the site, was given a new lease of life as a covered 'festival' shopping centre.

The other corner of the site for a while housed Edinburgh's tourist information office opposite the Festival and Tattoo offices across the road, but they were moved into the covered market.

The former fruit market on the south side was turned into an art gallery and café reached by a neat extension of the main railway platform footbridge from the main station. A larger warehouse on the opposite side of the road became the City Art Centre.

Railwayana

Original Waverley station (name was borrowed from Scott) was opened by the North British, June 22 1846. Extensively rebuilt and re-shaped from 1892 to 1902 when it was the largest of its type in Western Europe. The 19 platforms with through lines at either extremity gave it more platform accommodation than any other British station, Waterloo apart. Originally known as the General station, later becoming Waverley Bridge station and in 1854 acquiring its present name.

First extensions took place between 1869 and 1873, the NB hotel opened when the major rebuild was completed in 1902.

In 1970 a new travel centre opened and in 1979 new bookstall and alterations to the track were completed. Further improvements were made during the general eighties facelifts, including a line of shops by the northern through platform. Another recent major programme saw the replacement of the glazing of the very extensive roofing with toughened clear glass

An attempt by BR to rename the station simply 'Edinburgh' met with such opposition that it had to be 'abandoned' – but was it really?

Distances

London Kings Cross 394 ; Aberdeen 130; Dundee 59; Arbroath 77; Glasgow Queen Street 47; Glasgow Central (via Shotts) 47 – although strangely the same distance, time taken can be almost twice as long as for the Q. Street route.

Departures
19:11 Platform 17
Kirkcaldy
Calling at: Page 1 of 1
Haymarket (19:15)
South Gyle (19:20)
Dalmeny (19:26)
North Queensferry (19:30)
Inverkeithing (19:33)
Dalgety Bay (19:37)
Aberdour (19:42)
Burntisland (19:46)
Kinghorn (19:50)
& Kirkcaldy (19:58)
ScotRail
REAR 2 COACHES

Departures
19:15 Platform 18
Glasgow Queen St
Calling at: Page 1 of 1
Haymarket (19:19)
Linlithgow (19:35)
Polmont (19:41)
Falkirk High (19:46)
& Glasgow Queen St (20:09)
ScotRail

Departures
19:20 Platform 15
Glenrothes
Calling at: Page 1 of 1
Haymarket (19:24)
Edinburgh Gateway (19:29)
Dalmeny (19:35)
North Queensferry (19:39)
Inverkeithing (19:43)
Rosyth (19:47)
Dunfermline Town (19:51)
Dunfermline QM (19:55)
Cowdenbeath (20:01)
Lochgelly (20:07)
Cardenden (20:11)
& Glenrothes (20:21)
ScotRail

Departures
19:22 Platform 11
Helensburgh Ctl via
Calling at: Page 1 of 2
Haymarket (19:28)
Edinburgh Park (19:31)
Uphall (19:40)
Livingston North (19:42)
Bathgate (19:48)
Armadale (19:53)
Blackridge (19:57)
Caldercruix (20:03)
Drumgelloch (20:07)
Airdrie (20:10)
Coatbridge Sunny (20:14)
High St (20:25)
ScotRail

Departures
19:24 Platform 4
Tweedbank
Calling at: Page 1 of 1
Brunstane (19:32)
Newcraighall (19:35)
Shawfair (19:38)
Eskbank (19:43)
Newtongrange (19:46)
Gorebridge (19:50)
Stow (20:08)
Galashiels (20:15)
& Tweedbank (20:21)
ScotRail
Borders Railway

Departures
19:25 Platform 2
Stirling
Calling at: Page 1 of 1
Haymarket (19:29)
Falkirk Grahamston (19:54)
& Stirling (20:15)

Reservation Level
HGFEDCB
Virgin Trains East Coast
at seat service.
led due to a fault on this

Departures
19:27 Cancelled
Glasgow Central via
Calling at: Page 1 of 2
Haymarket
Slateford
Kingsknowe
Hester Bailes
Curriehill
Kirknewton
Livingston South
West Calder
Addiewell
Fauldhouse
Shotts
Hartwood
ScotRail

Departures
19:30 Platform 10
Glasgow Queen St
Calling at: Page 1 of 1
Haymarket (19:35)
Falkirk High (20:00)
Croy (20:10)
& Glasgow Queen St (20:24)
ScotRail
No 1st class available.

Departures
19:33 Platform 14
Dunblane
Calling at: Page 1 of 1
Haymarket (19:38)
Edinburgh Park (19:44)
Linlithgow (19:56)
Polmont (20:02)
Falkirk Grahamston (20:05)
Camelon (20:12)
Larbert (20:18)
Stirling (20:27)
Bridge of Allan (20:32)
& Dunblane (20:38)
ScotRail

The increasing powers of steam ...
will I think one day waft friends
together in the course of a few hours

Sir Walter Scott
cityofliterature.com #waverley200

Edinburgh Waverley

ELGIN
IV30 1QP (Moray)

Guidelines
As with many other parts of Scotland, the Beeching cuts dealt a heavy blow to rail links in the North East. Many of the branch lines that fed into the system at Elgin were axed, with the result that the town lost one of its two stations. Today's station, formerly known as the West station survived, while the East station which served lines to the coast, was closed.

The West station, which had originally opened in 1858, was replaced by a modern building *(see below)* in 1990. Gaining a Lidl store as a neighbour has helped compensate for the station's slightly removed position from the centre of town and has brought new life to the area.

The substantial East station *(see facing page, below)* lost all services but has found a new life as a business centre.

Railwayana
Plans for investment along the Aberdeen-Inverness line, including signalling upgrades, some station rebuilds and some timetable improvements should bring increased traffic to the line. Some services run beyond Aberdeen to Edinburgh and the timetables regularly show some services that continue beyond Inverness to Kyle of Lochalsh.

Distances
Inverness 37; Huntly 31; Inverness 71

As the name suggests it is pretty high up on a hill overlooking Falkirk. Only reason for getting off here would be a sudden change of mind en route between Glasgow and Edinburgh, though the car park is reasonably spacious if you like driving half way – and can find a space!

Railwayana

Opened by Edinburgh & Glasgow Railway, February 21 1842. The 'High' was first added to the station's sign boards on February 1 1903. The stone neo-classical building designed under the direction of John Miller was obliterated in 1980 and replaced by a modular box whose mansard roof and yellow brickwork retain a certain high Victorian flavour. Before this happened, in 1971, a platform shelter, made of anodised aluminium was, apparently, flown over from Toronto, difficult though this may seem to believe

Distances

Glasgow, Queen St. 21 miles; Edinburgh, Wav. 25 miles.

FEARN
IV20 1RS (Highland)

Guidelines
Fearn might have shared in development of oil platform construction at nearby Nigg, but despite occasional evidence of some pipe work, Fearn benefited little from this particular part of the oil 'boom.'

Back in the C16 the local abbey was quite a place, boasting nave, choir and several chapels. However in 1742, when the abbey had become the parish church, the roof chose an unfortunate time to fall in – a Sunday. More then 40 worshippers perished.

Elegant station house now a private dwelling recalling the estate office on a prosperous home farm.

Railwayana
Opened by Inverness & Aberdeen Jct. April 1 1864. Similar in style to Ardgay, Alness (demolished) and Kildary (closed). Victorian clock (long stopped) by Ferguson, Inverness – and the attractive porter's handcart in the picture above long since gone, along with the sign, too.

Distances
Inverness 41 miles; Wick 121 miles; Thurso 113 miles.

Strath Halladale, at the head of which Forsinard lies, saw some of the worst of the Clearances. Deserted crofts here and along the Strath of Kildonan, towards Helmsdale, recall the flourishing communities the area once supported.

Today Forsinard has become something of a birder's paradise. Not only has the station become an RSPB interpretive centre, but a twitchers' accommodation block has been built right opposite the 'For Sale' (former?) Forsinard Hotel.

Clearly not all Forsinard's few inhabitants share the birders' enthusiasms, as a sign in evidence at the entrance to the village *(see left)* at one time indicated.

Station Cottage, just to the south of the crossing, offers seasonal teas.

Railwayana

Opened by Sutherland and Caithness Railway, July 28 1874. There was a plan to continue down to Melvich on the north coast with a light railway, but though materials were delivered to Forsinard, a start was (fortunately!) never made.

As late as 1981 the water crane (minus canvas hose) used for steam engines was still in position. In summer the signal box would have a rare display of potted plants. Like many other stations in the far north a vemacular 'croft' style of building was employed.

Distances

Inverness 126 miles; Wick 36 miles; Thurso 28 miles.

FORT WILLIAM
PH33 6TQ (Highland)

Guidelines
The station once occupied pride of place bang in the centre of town, but the road planners decreed a by-pass and the railway was forced to retreat to a new purpose built 'transport centre' in the mid 70s. This was probably only fair since when it first got there at the end of the 19th century the railway had demolished what was left of the old fort which gave the town its name.

Today a few stretches of wall remain across the car park from said transport centre.

Best destination for the historically-minded is the West Highland Museum in Cameron Square in the centre of town – a splendid free enterprise effort. Dominating the square for a while was a purpose built information centre, complete with built-in cinema. Alas this closed early in the 21st century.

Welcome recent addition to the town's High Street, the Highland Bookshop, promoted by the owners of the Watermill in Aberfeldy, winner of national and international bookselling awards.

On the station concourse itself look out for the station bookstall, run for many years as Bill's Place by, you've guessed it, Bill himself!

Railwayana
Opened W Highland August 7 1894 (officially August 11). New station: June 13 1975. Major re-furbishment: 2007. Since 1984 starting point for ever-popular 'Jacobite' summer/autumn steam excursions to Mallaig – booking essential.

Distances
Glasgow 122; Mallaig 41; London, Euston 521

GARVE
IV23 2QF (Highland)

Guidelines
Like many a Highland village, Garve today boasts little in the way of public facilities. Hotel much favoured by summer tour parties has public bar with food open all year and swanky dining room on the go until all hours in the summer.

Just by the level crossing *(shown left, with steam meeting diesel)* an enterprising mobile trader set up to offer sustenance to the hungry traveller.

From Garve it may be possible to take an express bus to Ullapool home of the excellent Ceilidh Place – for good food, music and the spirit of the ceilidh. (Plans for a branch line – the Garve & Ullapool Railway – were never, alas, realised.)

Railwayana
Opened by Dingwall & Skye Railway, August 10 1870. Typical Dingwall & Skye station house and parcels office, probably dating (with footbridge) from early days of this century.

Unusually wide gap between up and down lines sad reminder of an ambitious scheme to transport fishing boats cross-country in competition with the Caledonian Canal. All the necessary widening of cuttings etc. was undertaken and the cranes required to lift the boats were put on order — but lack of funds prevented the hare-brained scheme from ever seeing the light of day.

Distances
Inverness 30 miles; Kyle of Lochalsh 52 miles; Ullapool (by the line they never built) 34 miles.

GEORGEMAS JUNCTION
KW12 6HH (Highland)

Guidelines

Not so busy, it has to be admitted, as Clapham Junction but a proper junction nonetheless and, by a very long margin, the most northerly one in Britain.

The oil boom brought some dramatic changes to Georgemas, as seen in the picture top left, when the goods yard became, for a while, a hectically busy pipe yard. This, following on from some lesser freightliner activity with clever inter-modal supermarket container transport.

More traditional scenes are enacted less frequently, with the (very) occasional summer visit of steam excursions – as when the Great Britain IX visited Thurso *(bottom left – and see also under Thurso)*.

Georgemas is, arguably, the nearest rail-head for attacking the lively Lyth Arts Centre. (Tel. 01955 641 434). Well worth a summer season visit.

Railwayana

Opened by Sutherland & Caithness Railway, July 28 1874.

Distances

Inverness 148 miles; Wick 14 miles; Thurso 7 miles; London, King's X 729 miles.

Glasgow Central

GLASGOW CENTRAL
G1 3SL

Guidelines
Claimed to be amongst the busiest rail termini in Britain, Glasgow Central is without doubt the most fascinating. Though a comparative youngster (it opened for business only in 1879), has wealth of intriguing details.

Repeated re-modellings and facelifts have ensured that facilities keep up with demand. The huge main concourse has allowed the complex to enjoy the advantages of the latest retail revolution, providing what is effectively a covered shopping centre. This been exploited by letting concessions to an ever-increasing number of eating places and boutiques.

Its clever design, on a level above surrounding streets, gives easy access to the very heart of the city, with a whole host of shops occupying what is effectively the lower parts of the station.

Privatisation succeeded in removing most of the charm of the Central Hotel, one of the stalwarts of the old British Transport chain. (Hotel actually started out as railway offices!) The hotel's Malmaison Restaurant was once a Glasgow dining legend. But even lurches from one owner to another did not manage to remove all the internal charm.

Railwayana
Prior to opening of Central, services terminated over the river at long-departed Bridge Street station. When a rail bridge was built (the first one was finished in 1878) it opened the way for the new station. First version, with just eight platforms, was far too small for the traffic generated and by the turn of the century something much grander was required. This was provided in the vision of the Caledonian Railway's engineer, Donald Matheson, whose far-sighted design produced, from 1901-6, today's station.

A second bridge was built over the Clyde, four more platforms and much more space added, curved building lines cleverly countering crowd build-up. Also introduced: the splendid train information indicator, only retired in the mid-eighties by BR. Happily stylish wooden housing was retained. Vehicle access also changed, though cars and taxis could still get close to the action.

Suburban travel available through the Low Level station, re-opened 1979, but subject to flooding on a number of occasions since then.

For ongoing travel to or from Edinburgh a direct service (saving changing stations from the more conventional Queen Street) though the same mileage, takes considerably longer.

Distances
Euston 401; Birmingham New St. 296; Bristol 385; Manchester 223; Liverpool 227; Carlisle 102; Stranraer 99; Edinburgh Waverley (via Shotts) 46; Gourock 26.

GLASGOW QUEEN STREET
G1 3SL

Guidelines

If Central is the station for coming and going (over the Border), Queen Street is the one for setting off on your journey of discovery in Scotland. It's from here that you depart for those romantic outposts of the West Highland line (culminating in Mallaig); Oban and the islands; Inverness and the far north; Dundee and Aberdeen and, on the hour and the half hour (at least), the capital city, Edinburgh.

Queen Street has never had the volume of traffic that Central enjoys, so except when two or three trains are arriving or departing together there is rarely the bustle that you so often get at Central.

But it's not badly placed for the city, being bang on George Square and very handy for the shops of Buchanan Street or Sauchiehall Street. Well worth a visit are the marbly splendid City Chambers on the east side of George Square; also nearby: Strathclyde University and a number of further education colleges.

Lacking the space of Central, QS has had little opportunity to promote retailing on the scale of the former. Concessions are limited to the usual bookstalls, an instant shoe repairers, fast food and eating and drinking facilities. (At one stage the complex was reputed to be BR's biggest catering venture).

The adjacent ex-British Transport Hotel (it used to be the North British) went through the usual rapid succession of owners since BR were told to sell it off. One enterprising Egyptian boss did much to improve facilities before selling out in apparent exasperation at the lack of support from bodies such as the Scottish Tourist Board – or VisitScotland as they became.

Railwayana

Oldest station left in operation within the city of Glasgow, Queen Street was opened on February 18 1842 as the western terminus of the Edinburgh & Glasgow Railway. Though not then electrified it was claimed at one time to be the second-busiest intercity route in Britain – an assertion not difficult to dispute during the morning and evening rush hours.

Notable feature of Queen Street station (apart from its 450 by 250 foot tied arched roof – *(see exterior view top left)* is a punishing incline (in a tunnel) which trains using the station must negotiate. For a long time a massive stationary engine hauled trains on a five inch rope, but eventually it was realised that locomotives could be made powerful enough to do the jobs themselves.

Low level station has electric (formerly Blue Train) services to Helensburgh and Balloch in the west and Airdrie in the east.

Distances

Inverness 180 miles; Mallaig 165 miles; Aberdeen 154 miles; Ft. William 123 miles; Oban 101m; Edinburgh 47m.

GLENCARRON (PLATFORM)

Guidelines
Glencarron, hidden away down a steep leafy track – the entrance is still just visible from the road – though now definitely and finally closed, merits inclusion in this guide as one of those wonderful anomalies that make this subject so engaging.

Along with a number of, particularly Highland, stations, Glencarron Halt started life as a private station for the local laird, a Mr Shaw of Glencarron Lodge. Eventually it found its way into the timetables, but like nearby Duncraig, it then disappeared, only to maintain a 'ghost' existence with trains stopping unofficially to set down or pick up.

The celebrated man of the outdoors, Tom Weir, recalls in his original guide, *The Kyle Line,* "running down to the Halt to pull the hand signal and stop the 'up' train..."

Unlike Duncraig, which came back to life in 1975, Glencarron remained in limbo, with some trains still unofficially stopping into the 90s. Today it is well and truly closed.

Railwayana
Opened 1873 as a private halt for nearby Glencarron Lodge. Opened as a public station 1887. The 'Platform' was dropped in 1962 *(see sign below)* and a couple of years later, in 1964, Dr Beeching got his way and closed it for good – except.... see above.

Distances
Dingwall 36 miles; Achnasheen 8 miles; Kyle of Lochalsh 28 miles

GLENEAGLES
PH3 1JL (Perth & Kinross)

Guidelines
In grander times there was a handy branch line to the famous hotel (and on to Crieff). When this closed there was a courtesy bus (phone from the station – *see left*). (Today's hotel guest *might* still be able to persuade reception to send a car.)

In the good old British Transport days even if you couldn't stand a full meal in the hotel, a drink at the old bar or their afternoon tea was a rare treat. Changed ownerships have introduced a more corporate style and plenty of conferencing. Indoor sports centre is impressive.

Auchterarder (1 mile) has some interesting shops — antiques in an old cinema, plus knitwear in the main street.

Railwayana
Opened as 'Crieff Junction' by Scottish Central Railway 1847, renamed April 1, 1912 and rebuilt 1919 for the Caledonian Railway. Station, footbridge and even the car park wall all B listed! Original four platforms now reduced to two and, of course, buffet, taxi rank and bookstall long since closed.

Hotel built 1924 for Caledonian Railway on the inspiration of general manager Donald Mathieson. The golfer James Braid was taken on to design the hotel's two golf courses and since then two more have been added. During World War II the hotel was used as a hospital.

A major facelift and fresh paint job was done to co-incide with the holding of the Ryder Cup in 2014.

For many years Gleneagles boasted non-standard signs. Very nifty maroon and cream numbers placed at right angles to the line to tempt the passing turista.

Distances
Glasgow, Queen Street 47 miles; Edinburgh, Waverley 54 miles; Aberdeen 108 miles; Inverness 134 miles; London, Euston 434 miles

Guidelines

With its museum, shop, dining AND sleeping cars, Glenfinnan is a very rare find among 'unstaffed' rural stations. All of it, of course, thanks to private initiative and enthusiasm. During the Jacobite steam season (extending by the year) station is a hive of activity when trains call – they allow time to visit and shop. Check website *(glenfinnanstationmuseum.co.uk)* for dining car hours and for booking a comfy overnight berth in the sleeping car.

Signed walks from the station lead out across the hills to the magnificent monument to poured concrete – the Glenfinnan Viaduct, much beloved of that seasoned young rail traveller, Master H. Potter.

Railwayana

Opened April 1 1901. Typical Swiss style WH station, two platforms, waiting room, now museum and shop. Signal box *(seen left, with snow-clad Ben Nevis catching the evening sun)* developed as interpretive/teaching centre.

Amongst impressive railway 'street furniture' on the campus, a snowplough and a stylish crane.

Distances

Fort William 17 miles; Mallaig 25 miles; Glasgow, Queen Street 140 miles.

HAYMARKET
EH12 5EY (City of Edinburgh)

Guidelines
The coming – eventually – of the trams to Edinburgh brought a whole new status to Haymarket station. With a tram stop right oustide the station just beside several bus stops, overnight it became a major transport interchange. The old DSS office block opposite the station became a budget hotel (£3 extra for a towel), M & S food set up on the spacious station concourse and a rash of cranes all around indicated there was much more to come.

Railwayana
Opened February 21 1842 as eastern terminus of Edinburgh & Glasgow Railway – Waverley was not reached till 1846. Believed to be second oldest operational through-passenger station in UK, with more or less intact main buildings. Apart from clock put in by NB in 1866, façade completely unchanged. Original trainshed, an elaborate cast and wrought iron structure, carefully dismantled 1982/3 for re-erection by Scottish Railway Presn. Socy. at their Bo'ness base.

Major rebuilding behind the unspoiled frontage at the time of the trams involving the lifting in place *(see middle picture, left)* of whole new sections of steel structure *(see top picture, left)* providing new escalators, lifts and a grand concourse, complete with bike hire!

Distances
Edinburgh, Waverley 1 mile; Glasgow, Queen Street 46 miles

HELMSDALE
KW8 6HH (Highland)

Guidelines
This was the northern end of the Duke of Sutherland's private railway, later incorporated into the Highland route on to Wick. Road and rail part company now at Helmsdale, the line striking inland to the Strath of Kildonan while the road bravely strikes up along the cliffs, part of the Ord of Caithness.

Helmsdale itself was founded in 1818 by Sutherland estates to house tenants evicted by them from their crofts in Straths Ullie and Kildonan.

Down the hill from the station and just across the bridge over the Helmsdale is Timespan gallery/museum/visitor centre. Well worth a visit for background history and stimulating changing exhibitions – plus refreshments. Along the street, one or two cafés, hotels and plenty of b & bs.

Chiming granite clock overlooking the harbour is a moving memorial to the fallen of World War I.

Railwayana
Opened June 19 1873. Helmsdale West station (some three quarters of a mile south, on the coast) was original northern terminus of Duke of Sutherland's railway.

Helmsdale proper was built when the final northern haul was undertaken and the whole line was joined up. Two platforms, footbridge, general waiting room. Footbridge made by Rose Street Foundry, Inverness 1905.

In 2013 work began on a community project to turn the stationmaster's house (long deserted) into self catering accommodation for visitors to the area. The four bedroom unit can be taken for week or half week rentals and discounts are available for guests prepared to lend a hand with station maintenance, or who arrive by train or bike! More from: *http://helmsdalestation.co.uk*

Distances
Inverness 101 miles; Wick 60 miles; Thurso 52 miles.

Guidelines

Once very handily placed for those visiting the adjoining cattle market before it decamped to an out of town site. A half a mile or so walk in to town where you will find shops, hotels and the headquarters of the lively Deveron Arts project

Look out for Rizza's ice cream enterprise (founded 1914) which has busy wholesale and retail trade. Sadly the large Jaeger factory – 'Edinburgh, Glasgow, London, Paris, New York,' as its sign once boasted, is no more – not even in Huntly, where some 200 knitters once worked.

On the platform, a post box once claimed three collections a day – not, alas, today.

Railwayana

Opened by Great North of Scotland Railway for goods traffic September 12 1854 — passengers had to wait another week. Unassuming wooden buildings dating from early 1890s *(see below and bottom left)* replaced by anonymous – but staffed! – waiting room/ticket office *(see top pictures left)*.

Two platforms connected by a remarkable footbridge made from old rails. Wooden mounting block once kept ready for the arrival of VIPs — or very short people *(see below)*.

Distances

Inverness 68 miles; Aberdeen 41 miles.

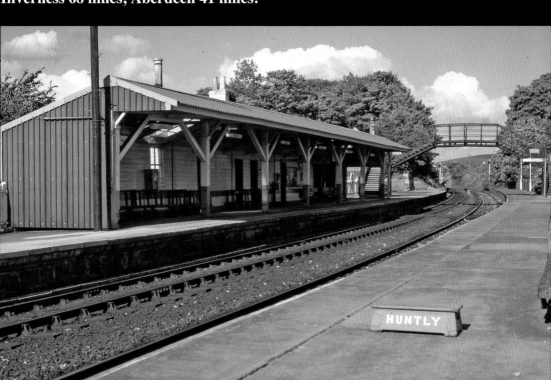

INSCH
AB52 6PU (Aberdeenshire)

Guidelines

Not quite at the heart of this burgh, but not a bad place to take a break. Rothney Arms (ex-Railway) Hotel right opposite offered 11am - 11pm welcome in summer. Half a mile into town for snacks, meals and gifts, but alas no longer Russell's of Insch, for an instant suit of tweeds! Clydesdale (formerly the North of Scotland) Bank once maintained unusually impressive presence, but now no sign of either.

Churchyard has 1613 belfry (and bell), while surveying all from on high is the ruined C13 Castle of Dunideer.

Railwayana

Opened, like neighbouring Huntly, September 12 1854 by Great North of Scotland Railway – but just for goods! As at Huntly, passengers had to wait another week.

Two platforms and a neat footbridge made up from rails. Present building proudly proclaims its 1880 ancestry and is one of best preserved examples of GNSR architecture.

Waiting room once offered touching 'bring and buy' selection of chairs, and some local art. Clock (silent) by Wilson of Keith; drinking fountain (dry) by Kennedy of Kilmarnock. Community museum and bookshop in main building.

Distances

Inverness 80 miles, Aberdeen 27 miles.

INVERGORDON
IV18 0NJ (Highland)

Guidelines
In the mid-eighties Invergordon seemed to be the centre of the oil business. No fewer than three rigs were parked bang outside the station, towering over cottages in the main street. A rig repair yard was doing a bomb.

A welcome break for the town still numbed by closure of the massive aluminium smelter abandoned early in its life after losing a fortune in recklessly subsidised electricity charges.

Station is handy for the main street with hotels, pubs and emporia. Nothing marks Invergordon's arguably greatest claim to fame, World War I mutiny which lent the town brief national notoriety. (Now Inverg. is a popular stop with cruise liners, thanks to deep water berthing.)

Railwayana
Opened by Inverness & Aberdeen Jct. March 21 1863.

Two platforms, fine footbridge and unusually pretty awning with delicate floral cast iron brackets. From the outside station could be taken for an estate office or a stable block.

Of special interest is the curvilinear or Dutch gable *(seen below)* above main entrance, rarely – if ever – found on Scottish railway premises of this date.

Murals – decorating the station and the town – the work of the enterprising Invergordon Off the Wall group, an initiative aimed at raising the profile of the town.

Distances
Inverness 32 miles; Wick 130 miles; Thurso 123 miles, Inverness 80 miles, Aberdeen 27 miles.

INVERKEITHING

KY11 1NJ (Fife)

Guidelines

Agricola slept here – but probably not in the waiting room.

Canny commuters to the capital city once saved their road bridge tolls by going by rail and this justified a major rebuild at InverK.

This is the station if you want an insider's view of the centenarian rail bridge – still one of the wonders of the railway world. A ticket to Dalmeny (q.v.) and back would do the trick – and you get two road bridges thrown in.

Station is quite well situated for town. Worth catching in the summer is the Lammas Fair which takes over the main street. Highland games in the summer down by the waterfront where they used to break up ships.

Railwavana

Opened by North British Railway, June 1890. Brick and wood buildings remained remarkably unchanged for nigh on a century before everything made way for a new structure on a rather more generous site.

In 1906 there were six private sidings here, today there are none. Just prior to the rebuild a unisex loo was espied, while on an earlier visit geraniums were seen growing in truncated hanging bottles. More useful to commuters is a handy news kiosk, just beside the ticket window.

Distances

Edinburgh, Waverley 13 miles; Aberdeen 117 miles; Perth 45 miles; London, King's Cross 406 miles

INVERNESS
IV2 3PY

Guidelines

Rightly regarded as the capital of the Highlands, Inverness is also at the hub of its railway system. You change here for pretty well anywhere you want to go to. And the station is bang in the middle of town.

Sadly, the developers did their best to destroy the old town – a process which has continued almost until the present. A particular eyesore was the HQ of the old Highlands and Islands Development Board in an uninspired concrete box beside the river. Only the plucky Inverness Courier remained (for a while) to show what has been lost. Worth a visit – the Museum & Art Gallery and, just facing the red sandstone Castle, the vibrant Castle Gallery.

The Station Hotel, a B listed building probably designed by Joseph Mitchell, with extensions by Matthews and Lawrie, was opened along with the station in 1855. Like all the other railway hotels it has suffered the indignity of being hawked off to private ownership, though the exercise seems to have been happier here than in many another former British Transport Hotel.

It's still a fine place for a quiet read – WH Smith maintain an excellent bookstall on the main concourse – and a pot of tea.

Railwayana

Opened by Inverness & Nairn Railway, November 5 1855.

The seven-platform terminal layout is unique, being formed along the two sides of a triangle, the other side being a through line linking north and south. There have been many changes over the years. In October 1876 the Highland Railway authorised Matthews & Lawrie to design a £3,700 extension to the hotel and at the same time they ordered their own engineers to design a £3,000 'new arcade and anival platform.'

There have been many subsequent modifications and alterations right up to the mid-1980s, when EU/EEC money helped many of Scotland's stations to undergo cosmetic surgery. Inverness, like many of the other larger Scottish stations was treated to a new terrazzo floor which did a lot to brighten the appearance of the place.

On the station concourse there are plaques celebrating the old Inverness & Aberdeen Junction Railway coat of arms and its chief big-wigs. Also to be seen is an old station bell bearing the inscription "I & AJR, 1858, Wilson Christie, Bellfounders, Glasgow."

Distances

Aberdeen 108 miles; Perth 118 miles; Edinburgh, Waverley 188 miles; Glasgow Queen St. 180 miles; Kyle of Lochalsh 82 miles; Wick 162 miles; Thurso 154 miles; London, Euston 568.

Opposite: Busy scenes after the arrival of a London train; lower pic: steam special for Kyle

INVERSHIN
IV27 4ET (Highland)

Guidelines
For long after it burned down, Invershin was a sorry sight. The original croft-like building remained roof-less for a number of years then a standard issue concrete block bus shelter went up. Old station house has been privatised and access is now by a track beside the old road.

The good news is the Invershin Hotel, open throughout the day for snacks, meals and a drink and as friendly a hostelry as you could hope to come across. For long a favourite stop for the fish lorries that plied on the route up to the far north west – look out for splendid photo-montage of boats and crews in the bar.

Reaching imposing Carbisdale Castle across the River Oykel *(seen sunlit in bottom picture),* no longer a youth hostel since its sale to the private sector, once required taking arguably Scotrail's shortest trip, the half mile across the Oykel to Culrain, but since a footbridge *(see top picture)* was cleverly bolted on to the side of the lattice girder bridge it's been a stroll.

Railwayana
Opened April 18 1868 by Sutherland Railway. Adjoining (virtually) B listed Oykel Viaduct, built 1867 to design of Joseph Mitchell and Murdoch Paterson. Iron lattice girder with 230 ft span.

Distances
Inverness 62 miles; Wick 100 miles; Thurso 92 miles.

Guidelines

North sea oil activity has proved some compensation for closure of the old loco works, source of many a fine Great North of Scotland locomotive. But as in many other locations, manufacturing has given over to retail and residential, both of which are much in evidence in modern day Inverurie. The distinctive loco works has been turned into nifty house units, with the name living on in a local café.

The station itself also boasts a popular coffee house with some on-the-platform lineside tables, cleverly calling itself the Coco Works.

Plenty of shopping opportunities in the nearby streets, including that increasing rarity, a proper newsagent/bookseller – with coffee and ice cream thrown in for good measure.

Railwayana

Opened to goods and passengers by Great North of Scotland Railway, September 12 and 19 1854 respectively. Original three platforms reduced to two and only main station buildings survive – the ubiquitous BR bus shelter adorning far platform, reached by a footbridge. Fine wood panelling, suffering some neglect, in general and ladies' waiting rooms and some nice architectural touches in the granite stone work.

An omate drinking fountain still graces the platform, planted with flowers in a fine summer. Local taxis usually maintain a strong presence outside.

Distances

Inverness 92 miles; Aberdeen 17 miles. In the past some London-Inverness 125s have been known to be routed through Inverurie, while many Edinburgh and some Glasgow bound Sprinters start and end their journeys here.

KEITH
AB51 9TNF (Moray)

Guidelines
Keith Station, or Keith Junction as it used to be called, is not as handy as it might be for the town of Keith. It's fine if you're planning a distillery visit (Strathisla, one of the oldest in Scotland, is just up the road), but it's a fair old haul to the town itself. When you get there it's essentially a one (narrow) street affair, with one or two fine old fashioned shops, and a few better known high street names.

Railwayana
Opened August 18 1858 by the Inverness & Aberdeen Junction Railway. Original four platforms have been unceremoniously reduced to one, for a long while incongruously known as Platform 4!

     In the days when Keith really was a junction trains sped off in all directions – the whisky line to Craigellachie, the fish line to Buckie. Through a commendable 1980s initiative, life was brought back to the whisky line through a summer excursion train, the Northern Belle, which ran from Aberdeen through Keith to the old Dufftown station. Since then the whisky line has been saved by volunteers.

     Sadly the link to the national system has been broken, but a smartly re-created Keith Town station *(see left)* offers summer and weekend services to the restored Dufftown station. *(Details: www.keith-dufftown-railway.co.uk)*

     From the outside Keith Junction in its heyday looked uncannily like a poorhouse, with the station agent's dwelling doing service as the 'Master's' house. Then the demolition squad moved in and now it's not much more than a superior bus shelter, having even lost its attractive canopy *(shown still in existence below)*.

Distances
Inverness 55 miles; Aberdeen 53 miles – half way house.

KILDONAN
KW8 6HY (Highland)

Guidelines
Not one of the systems's busiest stops – indeed one of the quietest on the whole network. with passenger figures sometimes apparently below three figures in a year.

Nearest habitation, a shooting lodge for which it was originally constructed, is some half a mile away and, apart from that, there appears to be very little sign of life at all.

In 1868-9 a flurry of activity came to the strath with the 'gold rush.' Reports of a find in the Kildonan Burn brought prospectors from all parts, but though some £6000 worth was actually found it was regarded as uneconomic and as suddenly as the rush had started it came to an end. One hundred years later there was a renewal of interest, but this too soon petered out.

Standing stones and cairns on nearby Learable Hill.

Railwayana
Opened by Sutherland & Caithness Railway July 28 1874. Kildonan today consists of a humble shed (locked) on the wrong side of the line and some elaborate provision for electric lights still awaiting connection when an investigator called. Unmanned and ungated level crossing.

Rather unbelievably, the station won an award in BR Scottish Region's Best Kept Stations category in the 1950s.

Distances
Helmsdale 10 miles; Inverness 111 miles; Wick 50 miles

KINBRACE
KW11 6UB (Highland)

Guidelines
Unlike neighbouring Kildonan station, where nothing at all seems to happen, Kinbrace remained for a while a real hive of activity... well!

The PO/store right by the station sold everything – and was the perfect place to put together an ad hoc picnic if you decided to get off here to explore Strath Naver, scene of some of the worst excesses visited on the area during the Clearances. But alas time and tide... now even the filling station seems to have closed, though some picturesque corrugated iron buildings survive.

A Post Bus service once ran through Strathnaver to Bettyhill on the coast passing the incredibly remote Garvault Hotel, which still advertises its presence at the road end.

During the 1870s there were some interesting attempts at land reclamation hereabouts using a steam plough, but no great success seems to have attended the experiment.

Railwayana
Opened by Sutherland & Caithness Railway July 28 1874. Like Forsinard next up the line, a charming cottage building with outside stairs serving upper storey, it has been converted to domestic use. Footbridge long since demolished and removed.

The concrete block 'station' *(just seen in the lower picture on the left)* – which incredibly once came equipped with Calor gas lighting – has been supplanted by the ubiquitous yellow bus shelter *(see picture below)*.

Distances
Wick 44 miles; Inverness 118.

Guidelines

After Burntisland, Kinghorn makes a pleasant change. Station overlooks, literally, a delightful sandy beach, making it just the place for a wee run out of Edinburgh. Right by the station, just over footbridge, the Pantry Restaurant with inspiring concrete legend '1936'. Just out on the road from the station are shops, PO and a bus stop.

      Under 'Shops information' for Kinghorn the Scotrail station website records: 'Artist studio.'

      Watch out when riding near Kinghom Ness on stormy nights: Alexander III did this in 1286 and there was no sign of him until 600 years later, in 1886, a Celtic cross was put up to 'mark the spot'. You have been warned!

Railwayana

Opened Edinburgh, Perth & Dundee Railway, September 17 1847. Two platforms and foot-bridge. Very domestic looking stone building is original, with waiting rooms and ticket office housed in a homely wooden extension, probably added c.1880 by the NB. As late as 1977 there was a sighting of 1847 gas lamps inscribed 'Edinr. & Perth Raily.'

      Over the way simple wooden shelter was formed by boxing in a still more simple wooden awning.

Distances

Edinburgh Waverley 23 miles; Arbroath 54 miles.

KINGUSSIE
PH21 1EN (Highland)

Guidelines
After it was first by-passed by the A9, Kingussie flourished, with a clutch of good places to eat and honourable mentions even in the Good Food Guide and Michelin. Also in town: a couple of galleries.

Station is quite handy for the town. Over River Spey and a mile out of town, ruined remains of old Ruthven Barracks, built to subdue the locals between 1715 and the '45 and burned down 1746 by B. Prince Charlie's supporters.

Not too far from town, the Highland Wildlife Park.

Railwayana
Opened Inverness & Perth Junction Railway, September 9 1863. Original station, for which drawings still survive, built by Gowans & Mackay, subsequently completely remodelled in plain neo-baronial idiom 1881 by William Roberts.

Grand structure which survives is listed B, dominated by very generous station master's house. Look out for Edward VII pillar box and ancient luggage barrow *(seen in picture bottom left, opposite)*, the latter surely long departed. Also pleasing decorated brackets supporting glazed awning over platform – not too common on Highland Railway.

Distances
Inverness 47 miles; Perth 72 miles; Glasgow, Queen St. 134 miles; Edin., Wav. 144 miles; London, Euston 521 miles.

KYLE OF LOCHALSH

IV40 8AH (Highland)

Guidelines

Kyle, as the locals call it, was given a new lease of life by oil-related development on the west coast and by the arrival, or rather the return, of the Navy. During the war Kyle – it was known as Port ZA for security reasons – played a major part in sea defences and the railway worked overtime carting materials, mines especially, plus thousands of troops from one ocean to the other.

Today, Kyle's principal importance is as main gateway to Skye. For many years a ferry service plied 18 heroic hours a day *(see picture below)*. Then came the bridge – first with tolls and then (after huge payoff to men in suits) toll-free – thanks in no small part to the efforts of one Robbie the Pict.

Despite its slight shanty town appearance, Kyle is a fine provisioning point well served by shops, (including a big Co-op), freelance tourist info and smart (charging) public loo in upper car park.

Principal among hotels is the Lochalsh, built and owned by the railways but sold off in early bout of Tory privatisation.

Railwayana

Opened, after a struggle to get there, with stops on the way at Strathcarron and Stromeferry November 2 1897 by the Highland Railway. Solid rock had to be carved out both to reach Kyle and to accommodate sidings and station, part of which extends out on a pier.

With the opening of the Ullapool-Stornoway ferry service Kyle lost its importance as a steamer terminal for the Western Isles.

Repeated economy drives and the ever present threat of closure left their mark on the station until the Friends of the Kyle Line took up the cause and opened an excellent shop and interpretive centre in the station. Also on the platform a sea-food restaurant – check opening times.

Handy phone kiosk (still?) and (rare) gents toilet on the platform. Station clock the work of one Alexander Mitchell, Glasgow.

Distances

Inverness 82 miles; Achnasheen 46 miles; Plockton 6 miles

Guidelines

Ladybank owes its existence as a burgh largely to the railway. The junction on the line where it branched to Perth or Dundee grew because of its rail link. But in 1955 passenger services on the Ladybank-Perth line were withdrawn, then amazingly 20 years later in 1975 a new straight through service to Inverness was instituted and the station came alive again.

Over the years the rather grand station buildings have had various uses, including a meeting place for the Ladybank ambulance section and, more recently, an ambitious local arts centre *(see top picture left)*.

Railwayana

Opened by Edinburgh Perth & Dundee Railway September 17 1847. Main station block is unusually A listed, with subsidiary buildings and railway work shop all B listed.

Italianate design achieves a most pleasing effect, with simpler wood and brick structure on the far platform *(see bottom picture, left)* providing sympathetic contrast.

Also at the junction impressive engine shed and office block with intriguing cast iron window frames with diamond panes. A must for the serious student of railway architecture.

Distances

Edinburgh, Waverley 39 miles; Aberdeen 92 miles; Inverness 136 miles.

LAIRG
IV27 4EX (Highland)

Guidelines
In the north of Scotland it's easy to gain misleading impressions. Lairg features in so many postal addresses that you might imagine it was quite a metropolis. It's not! Two or three hotels, a couple of shops and a very attractive loch.

Ah, but! Station is about a mile away from even this centre of civilisation, so unless you're prepared to walk you're probably better to stay on board. Unless, that is, you happened to be there the day of the autumn sheep sales. Historically one of the biggest in Scotland with tens of thousands of fleecy friends coming under the hammer. Changing times and the inexorable rise of the internet have reduced its importance. Once whole train loads of sheep would leave from the nearby pens.

Railwayana
Opened April 18 1868 by Sutherland Railway and enlarged 1872 and again 1875. Unassuming vernacular cottage style, characteristic of the line. Two platforms with originally a waiting room each and standard issue HR footbridge. For some perplexing reason the station clock's face had been obscured by a photograph of a Caledonian MacBrayne steamer when a station sleuth called.

Lairg was once famed as final destination of a Sunday paper special which ran all the way from London!

Distances
Inverness 67 miles; Wick 95 miles; Thurso 87 miles.

Guidelines

What comes closest to being the Crewe of Scotland, a well-kent junction for any traveller venturing to the north of Glasgow. Larbert itself joins on to Falkirk and only a purist would know where the seam was. But the town has its own centre and the station is near it.

For many years Larbert's main attraction was doubtless the Barbara Davidson Pottery up Muirhall Road, just by the station, but sadly now closed.

Railwayana

Opened in 1847 by Scottish Central Railway, but from July 5 1865 in the ownership of Caledonian Railway who bequeathed to LMS and then BR a pretty miserable little station.

In 1976 the convenor of the then Central Region, one James Anderson, presided over a grand opening ceremony for yet another new station on the site, a £100,000 brick and glass job complete with refurbished footbridge.

Half a mile to the S. the mighty B listed Larbert Viaduct crosses the River Carron. Engineer: Joseph Locke.

Distances

Glasgow, Queen Street 21 miles; Edinburgh, Waverley 28 miles; Aberdeen 133.

the St Andrews branch, leaving Leuchars high and dry. Amazingly this did not kill it off and a swarm of taxis meets most trains. Leuchars was renowned for its air base and for quite a while a siding existed, presumably to convey unspeakable armaments into the stronghold. Evidence still exists in the form of a couple of metres of rail stranded beside the main road at the point where the line entered the camp.

If you are of a more peaceable frame of mind, make for the C12 parish church about a mile north of station – breathtaking Norman carving.

Railwayana

Opened May 1848 by Edinburgh Perth & Dundee Railway. Heavily remodelled since then on various occasions, a notable and not altogether attractive feature being curious mansard roof clad in felt or asbestos shingles.

Iron columns and Gothic brackets bear an uncanny resemblance to those at Dundee station, and presumably date from late 1870s. Two through platforms.

Working tap (NBR) with legend 'Keep the pavement dry' at S. end of station disappeared after our first edition appeared – as did the two terminal platforms. Non-functioning Victorian clock by J. Ritchie & Sons, Edinburgh.

Distances
Edinburgh, Wav. 50 miles; Aberdeen 80 miles; London, King's X 444 miles.

UNION CANAL WALKWAY →

TO POLMONT STATION (VIA AQUEDUCT) 9km AND TO FALKIRK HIGH STATION (VIA AQUEDUCT AND TUNNEL) 15km

CROSS CAR PARK. AT EXIT, TURN RIGHT UP THE HILL. THE UNION CANAL IS 150m AHEAD.

RETURN BY TRAIN.

One of those places with a spectacular past and, if one is honest, a slightly boring present day reality. Though recent improvements have lifted the town, it's small beer compared with what must have been when Linlithgow Palace was on the go in the 15th and 16th centuries. Today, alas, Palace is but a ruin, but a pretty dramatic one at that. Building took place over 100 years from 1424 onwards.

Cumberland's troops occupied after the '45 and there was a mysterious fire shortly afterwards.

Railwayana
Opened February 21 1842 by Edinburgh & Glasgow Railway. Two platforms and a subway and at one time a special siding for prison trains! Heavily altered over the years both in late Victorian times and in the sixties, yet probably the best preserved through station on the line.

Amongst facilities claimed for the station when this edition went to press were: a 'unisex disabled toilet,' a car park with '91 spaces,' a taxi rank and 'cycle racks for 14 cycles' *(see picture left)*.

Distances
Glasgow, Queen St. 30 miles; Edin., Waverley 18 miles

Guidelines

During construction of the Mallaig Line, Lochailort was of paramount importance. A massive camp housed over 2000 navvies. There was a hospital, bakery and an enormous provision store.

Today all that is a bit difficult to believe. The station buildings have gone but at least there is still the Lochailort Inn to make you welcome

Right opposite the hotel, a charming tin tabernacle claiming to offer local kirk services "monthly as indicated at 3pm."

Careful time-tabling here can link you up with Shiel Buses *(www.shielbuses. co.uk)* for the wilds of Ardnamurchan and beyond!

Railwayana

Opened April 1 1901 by West Highland Railway and unstaffed since July 3 1967.

Once a fine example of the 'Swiss style' of West Highland station produced by 'Concrete Bob' McAlpine.

Alas, maintenance was non-existent and in the mid-1980s BR bulldozed the station and replaced it, short-sightedly, with one of their bus shelters, thereby losing the opportunity to add to the scenic attraction of the line by a little imaginative refurbishment – a policy more in keeping with the re-introduction of steam on the line – so long as it didn't set the heather on fire *(see middle picture)*.

Distances

Glasgow, Queen Street 149 miles; Mallaig 15 miles; Fort William 26 miles.

LOCKERBIE
DG11 2HA (Dumfries & Galloway)

Guidelines
Since the dreadful night of December 21 1988, Lockerbie has been known internationally for the Lockerbie Disaster – the bringing down of Pan Am flight 103 with the loss of 270 souls, including all those on board and 11 unlucky inhabitants of the town's Sherwood Crescent.

A moving memorial to those lost – the Lockerbie Memorial Garden of Remembrance – was established just outside the town at the Dryfesdale Lodge Visitors' Centre, which houses a small exhibition centre and a quiet room for reflection.

Life, however, goes on and Lockerbie benefits from having the only station remaining open between Carstairs on the outskirts of the Central Belt and Carlisle.

Railwayana
Opened September 1847 when the Caledonian Railway drove their line north from Carlisle as far as Beattock. A branch line to Dumfries, via Lochmaben, opened some 16 years later. Passenger services ran on it until 1952, but the line closed for good in 1966 when Doctor B. decreed that no more freight trains should run.

Electrification of the West Coast main line from Crewe to Glasgow brought speedier long distance services in 1974, but the great majority of the new trains rattled through the station at high speed.

Distances
Carlisle 26 miles; Glasgow Central 76 miles; Edinburgh Waverley 76 miles

MALLAIG
PH41 4QA (Highland)

Guidelines

This has always been the Road to the Isles, but with Caledonian MacBrayne policy you never know! In particular the ferry to Skye has sometimes found itself under threat. While it's going, make the most of it: using a bus from landing point, Armadale, a neat round trip effect can be achieved picking up the train again at Kyle. This part of Skye – the Sleat Peninsula – is well worth a visit from Mallaig. Armadale Castle is an easy walk from the ferry terminal and has an excellent visitor centre with eats and drinks. Or visit the Small Isles – a regular service takes in the islands of Rhum, Eigg, Muck & Canna.

Mallaig itself has lots to offer. Pubs, restaurants, shops and a handy free enterprise Tourist Info. The Co-op has an obliging habit of staying open late, useful if you arrive late in the day.

Wide range of hotels, including Marine right next to station. Though the Fishermen's Mission just opposite has ceased to be, a friendly café lives on there.

Railwayana

Opened, after a monumental struggle, April 1 1901. West Highland faced appalling problems first in getting necessary approvals, then backing and finally attracting the labour, but they did it and, miracle of miracles, the line is still open!

Station itself, only one on line with island platform, has undergone radical changes in recent years. First it lost its canopy, then its bookstall and looked set for closure, then a new travel centre opened, and then the return of summer steam.

In its heyday Mallaig would despatch a dozen or more fish specials a day. They left round the clock carrying tons and tonnes of herring to market. Then the line to the quayside was lifted and a new road cut off the station from the fishing boats.

After standing for many a year, the 'sea wall' shielding the station from the waves succumbed to the demolishers to accommodate the new road.

Ever keen to save a bob or two, BR removed the turntable, thus depriving the terminus of a great asset – steam engines could no longer be turned and attempts to restore one have proved longwinded, expensive and – so far – fruitless.

Distances

Glasgow, Queen Street 165 miles; Fort William 42 miles.

Guidelines

Whisky and paper are the two products you associate with Markinch and the former continues to flourish, even if the latter experienced some difficulties. The distillery – Haig's – adjoins the station; the paper mill is a bit farther afield.

Station itself had a major facelift at the turn of the century (the 21st, that is) and effectively decamped from the elegant domestic premises it originally occupied to a far more prosaic modern structure on rather flatter land beside the station *(see middle picture on the left)*.

St Drostan's Church dates from the 12th century. One and a half miles out of town, A listed Balgonie Castle is based on a C15 tower.

Railwayana

The original station was on two storeys, with the booking office on street level and a waiting room down below on platform level. There were awnings on cast iron columns on the upper and lower storeys. Station clock – one of the finest on any small station in Britain – made by the Bryson family of Edinburgh, important innovators in early Victorian horology. To the south look out for the Markinch Viaduct, a ten arch stone beauty.

Distances

Edinburgh, Waverley 33 miles; Aberdeen 97 miles.

MORAR
PH40 4PB (Highland)

Guidelines
Unlike many of the stations on the Mallaig line (and elsewhere) which BR allowed to crumble and then collapse, Morar was allowed to flourish, first as a pottery and subsequently as a bakery, then as a local newspaper office *(see picture, below left)*.

Since the first edition of this guide the bakery closed as also did the PO and general store just opposite. Large hotel and guest houses survive and Loch Morar is still thought to retain its resident monster 'Morag,' just down the road.

Railwayana
Opened with a flourish on April 1 1901 by the West Highland Railway but neglected for many a year thereafter until re-born to the sound of the potter's wheel, then the oven.

For a while near slapstick scenes were enacted at the level crossing just by the station. De-staffing left no one to operate the gates so train staff themselves had to do the job, stopping before and after to open and close big white gates. Alas, all this ended when natty flashing lights and jangling bells took over *(see opposite)*.

Distances
Glasgow, Queen St. 162 miles; Mallaig 2.5 miles; Fort William 39

1855 **2005**

INVERNESS & NAIRN RAILWAY

ON THE 5th. OF NOVEMBER 1855, THE FIRST RAILWAY LINE
IN THE HIGHLANDS WAS OPENED AND NAMED THE INVERNESS &
NAIRN RAILWAY. THE LINE WAS EXTENDED EAST TO ELGIN IN
1856, TO KEITH IN 1858 AND, BRANCHING SOUTH, TO PERTH
IN 1863. IT BECAME PART OF THE HIGHLAND RAILWAY IN
1865. THIS PLAQUE COMMEMORATES 150 yrs OF CONTINUAL
RAIL SERVICE TO THE ROYAL BURGH OF NAIRN.
UNVEILED BY THE COUNTESS OF SEAFIELD ON THE 9th. JULY 2005.

STEPHEN SEEDHOUSE
FLOWERS

NAIRN
IV12 4QS (Highland)

Guidelines
Well established as a holiday resort since Victorian times, drawing visitors from as far afield as London to its sandy beaches and rolling links (two 18-holers and one 9-holer). Fewer grand hotels than in its heyday (some have become retirement flats) and some, like the flamboyant Clifton, have closed their doors.

Station is not exactly on the sea front and indeed it's a wee bit of a walk to the main street and the shops. But it's worth it: Nairn has a flavour all its own and is a particularly Scottish institution. Canny operators could save a bob or two by alighting here for booming Inverness Airport – nearer Nairn than Inverness.

Definitely worth a detour to the coast is a trip to the Cheese Pantry just by Ardesier, one of the finest cheese retailers (and makers) in the country.

Railwayana
Opened as early as 1855 by Inverness and Nairn Railway and rebuilt by the Highland Railway 30 years later, now B listed and an attractive piece of Victoriana, probably the work of William Roberts.

Quite similar in appearance to Pitlochry station with crow-stepped gables and a recessed awning on cast iron columns.

East of the station look out for the B listed Nairn Viaduct, built by Joseph Mitchell in four stone spans *(see picture opposite)*.

Distances
Aberdeen 93 miles; Inverness 15 miles

NEWTONMORE
PH20 1AL (Highland)

Guidelines
Newtonmore seems to have suffered more acutely than some other communities by-passed by the A9 highway. There is a bit of an air of desolation about the main street and even Little Chef on the outskirts of town packed up and called it a day when the cars were re-routed – only for a smart operator to open a highly successful truck stop in its place.

It has to be said that Newtomnore station is not exactly bang in the middle of the village – it must be a good ten minute walk to the main street where you will find caffs a'plenty, Macpherson clan museum, antique shops and a sizeable Co-op.

Railwayana
Opened September 9 1863 by Inverness and Perth Junction Railway. Another well preserved example of a Highland Railway 'board school' style station house which proudly announces its date of birth, or rather rebuilding – 1893. Not quite so grand as, for example, Pitlochry or Nairn, but pretty nice nonetheless. As well as an Edward VII pillarbox, there used to be a wooden wheeled handcart of a pattern used by tradesmen in many Scottish towns until the late 1950s.

Top pictures on the left show station pre-conversion to a private house and, on the right, a new build house hard by showing interesting 'signal box' influence.

Distances
Inverness 49 miles; Perth 69 miles; Glasgow, Queen Street 132 miles; Edinburgh, Waverley 142 miles; London, Euston 519 miles

Welcome to North Berwick
Willkommen in North Berwick
Bienvenue à North Berwick

NORTH BERWICK

Guidelines

North Berwick is one of those places people always seemed to be going to in the 1930s. They obviously still go there – and probably for the same reasons. The golf courses, the homely hotels and boarding houses, the swimming pool, the sands – even boat trips to the Bass Rock.

The place has a history too: the C12 kirk of St Andrew; 'The Abbey' (near the station); the Town House and the Law – not the Boys in Blue but the hillock of that name rising to fully 612 ft.

Railwayana

Opened June 7 1850, courtesy of the North British and a rebuild of the original station took place in 1890, or then-abouts. All was going well until 1985 when the BR modernisation squad moved in (fresh from their 'successes' at Drem, where they tried to demolish the B listed station) and that was that! The old station *(shown in black and white on the left)* bit the dust, valanced curved awning and all.

British Railways had ordained that a new station should grace North Berwick, so 'grace it' it has – see picture below.

Popular commuter specials from the station began running all the way to Haymarket in the morning and back in the evening in 1979 – that's progress for you.

The strange multi-lingual welcome sign *(pictured top left),* displayed on the platform, is thought to predate the Brexit campaign by several years!

Distances

Drem 5 miles; Edinburgh, Waverley 22 miles

OBAN
PA34 4LW (Argyll & Bute)

Guidelines
Ferry arrangements are always a big issue in Oban. For quite a while most services left from the north pier and this meant a trudge through the town from the station. Latterly they have seemed settled at the railway pier, but you never know!

Main service is the roll-on roll-off 'liner' to Craignure on Mull – that's the one to get to go to Iona. But Oban has plenty other services too: to Coll and Tiree; to Colonsay, Lismore, Barra and Lochboisdale, and that is not to mention the clutch of private operators with 'trips round the bay.'

Oban itself has a strong Glasgow flavour to it, hardly surprising since it was folk from the central belt who made it. Today its visitors come from farther afield but it's still a pretty useful stopping point on the west coast.

The hotels and guest houses start where the shops end and sweep round as far as the eye can see. Gourmets will probably want to strike out for Eriskay, 12 miles north or even 10 miles on to Port Appin to discover two of Scotland's most highly rated hotels. Sadly, since closure of the Ballachulish branch it's impossible to go by train.

Railwayana
Reaching Oban was no mean achievement for the Callander & Oban Railway. They finally did it in 1880, the ceremonial opening being on June 30 and first passenger services the following day. Shortage of funds was one thing but the good burghers of Oban were not too helpful either – hence the fiendishly circuitous approach.

But the station they got *(bottom picture)* was like no other. Its wooden framing and exposed timbers gave the impression of an overgrown Swiss chalet and the clock tower could be seen for miles around.

One observer described it as 'an eclectic fantasy run up at moderate expense.' Part of the parcels office displayed a rare example of Victorian artificial stonework.

Not that all this availed much: BR in their wisdom saw fit to replace the fantasy with a much more down to earth, not to say cramped, off the shelf edifice *(seen in top picture with original station still standing)*. On the skyline in the middle picture the landmark McCaig's Tower, disrespectfully known as his Folly.

Distances
Glasgow, Queen Street 102 miles; Crianlarich 42 miles.

Perth

Guidelines

Not as well sited as it might be for the city centre but not bad. Station Hotel just across the forecourt. Like the other railway hotels, 'privatised' in recent years but prices are quite modest and service, while nowhere near the old British Transport standard, is not bad. Particularly missed is the immaculate BTH cocktail bar service which always had a Gallic flavour.

Not far from the station is the Queen's Hotel, also near at hand are a couple of Chinese carry-outs and a chip shop.

Perth has a swanky new concert hall, lively theatre, a first class butcher and a fish merchant, delicatessens – and is home of 'The Famous Grouse' – Matthew Gloag sell it and wines in panelled elegance on Kinnoull Street.

The town is also something of a gold mine for art and antique collectors – look out for a guide with a map to show the shops and galleries.

Railwayana

Opened September 17 1847, from 1863 onwards it was managed by the Perth General Station Joint Committee and catered for the Caledonian, North British and Highland Railways. Architects were Sir William Tite and Ebenezer Trotman, who designed Carlisle station (a copy of their elevations may be consulted in the Scottish Record Office). The similarities to Carlisle are most marked, with stone screen walls and the overall Tudor styling.

In its heyday Perth witnessed frenetic activity with as many as two dozen long-distance expresses disgorging passengers to join other trains at the busiest times. Today all that is sadly changed and only the Dundee platform has much activity.

On the whole of the central island, apart from ladies and gents and a waiting room, the only 'facility' appeared to be a chocolate vending machine – what a change from the days when dining rooms were crammed with travellers! There is a caff, open seven days a week, but that is situated by the entrance.

In the 60s BR carried out a sadly misguided tarting-up operation, damaging one of the most remarkable pre-1850 railway monumcnts in Scotland, but they then made some attempts to remedy the situation. The vandalised stone work at the entrance was restored and a superb paint job was done throughout.

Goods station was for long the best surviving example of an old goods complex in the country.

Distances

Edinburgh, Wav. 58 miles; Glasgow, Queen St. 63 miles; Aberdeen 92 miles; Inverness 118 miles; London, Euston 450 miles; Birmingham, New Street 345 miles.

PITLOCHRY
PH16 5AN (Perth & Kinross)

Guidelines

Always a favourite with the day trippers, Pitlochry now gets more of these by road than rail. But the station is well placed for the town, indeed Fisher's Hotel has a 'back door' that gives right on to it.

Shops are rather more of the touristic kind, though most necessities can be acquired and there is a range of moderately priced, if not wildly exciting, eating places. Tourist information on Atholl Road is a wee bit far from the centre of things, though the set-up is good enough.

A must on any summer visit to Pitlochry is a night out to the theatre. Built on hard graft and inspired local vision, Pitlochry Festival Theatre is a most impressive monument to single-minded dedication. The money to build the new theatre (it replaced one in a superior kind of garden shed) was almost entirely raised by local subscription and business sponsorship. A restaurant/tea room open through the day serves reasonably priced eats and there's a gallery and shop there too.

Also worth remembering in Pitlochry: a visit to one of the two distilleries in town. Best known is the Blair Athol, you see it from the train en route for Perth, but much more intriguing if you're feeling adventurous is a visit to the tiny Edradour distillery up in the hills behind town. Check out by phone, though, whether you'll be welcome.

Sadly missed is the Post Bus service that once meandered up the line to Dalnaspidal – the station's long since closed, but it's wild and woolly country.

Railwayana

First opened by Inverness and Perth Junction Railway on June 1 1863. Rebuilt by the Highland Railway in their elegant baronial style in 1882 and re-jigged in 1896 and on one or two occasions since then. Similar in many respects to the HR station at Nairn.

Appearance rather marred for a while by some weak modern lettering on the awning in the recess between the two gables. The Menzies bookstall closed in the Seventies, but 30 years later an enterprising local initiative re-opened it as a second hand bookshop. An ornate drinking fountain, complete with guarding heron, was to be found beyond the main station building, moved here from the old Strathyre station when it closed in 1969.

Drama came here as early as 1865 when on October 21 the 12.40 from Inverness collided with the 4.15 from Perth. Fortunately there was "no serious injury to passengers."

Distances

Inverness 90 miles; Perth 29 miles; Glasgow, Queen. St. 91 miles; Edinburgh, Wav. 101 miles; London, Euston 478 miles

Guidelines

Though the station is a little bit out of the village, that shouldn't discourage the rail-borne visitor because Plockton has a gentle charm that nowhere else on the west coast can really match.

A long established craft/bookshop, weaving workshop and a summer-time gallery, as well as a handful of hotels where you can always get a pint and a snack, or go further! An airstrip (for private fliers) is just by the station, beyond the nearby school.

Railwayana

Opened November 2 1897 mainly for the convenience of the Mathiesons of nearby Duncraig Castle, until their own private platform was opened just beneath the castle. Recent times have seen the station take on a new lease of life, offering, as 'Off the Rails' a lineside café *(see middle picture, left)* then subsequently, self-catering premises 'available for short lets.'

Plockton station is a fine example of a Highland Railway owned building with a slated awning supported by five Corinthian columns.

Design is similar to that of Carr Bridge, (built five years earlier, in 1892) which is far more easily seen. Plockton station hides away beneath the road bridge nearby *(see picture, bottom left)* and indeed can easily be missed from the road.

Distances

Inverness 77 miles; Kyle of Lochalsh 5 miles

RANNOCH
PH17 2QA (Highland)

Guidelines
One of the most romantic stations on the whole Scottish system. Not quite as remote as Corrour *(q.v.)*, but very isolated and bang in the middle of the moor of the same name. On the platform the excellent (and popular) station café, offering meals and refreshments and magnanimously offering a loo open to the public – contributions most welcome! (Closed Fridays).

Hard by the station is the Moor of Rannoch Hotel – it used to be The Station *(just seen right of the collapsed snow fence in the top picture, left)*. Seasonal accommodation and meals, but essential to book ahead.

Rannoch Moor itself should be treated with great respect. A path leads across to Kingshouse to join up with the West Highland Way, but striking out unprepared across the muir is not recommended. Early in the century many men were lost when they took the short cut over to Kinlochleven where they were building the aluminium smelter.

Railwayana
Opened August 3 1894. Standard pattern island platform buildings to the design of Charles Forman. At the north end of the platform an enormous boulder bears the carved head of a Mr Renton, a director of the West Highland Railway, who personally put up a large part of his own wealth to help the company over one of its bad times during construction. Navvies working on the line carried out the sculpture as a spontaneous gesture of gratitude.

Construction problems on this section were appalling. Bog conditions threatened to submerge the line and thousands of tons of soil, ash and brushwood needed to be laid to create a firm footing.

Just north of the station is the longest bridge on the line, a nine-span steel viaduct by Lucas & Aird. This too posed great problems when it came to finding sure foundations, though the granite for the piers came conveniently from the nearby Cruachan cutting.

Distances
Glasgow, Queen Street 87 miles; Mallaig 77 miles; Fort William 36 miles; London, Euston 489 miles.

Viewed from the line
One mile N. of station is Cruachan snow shed, covering the line at its most exposed summit – now, alas, a large expanse of rather sorry rusty corrugated.

Travelling south try to catch a glimpse of disused Gorton Station now little more than a passing loop – where, in an old carriage, a railway school was maintained for many years.

Guidelines

The land around Rogart is much more like the W. Highlands than East, an impression strengthened by the presence of so many crofting holdings.

Rogart itself has a dignity and charm all its own. Hotel was for long a bastion of sound good sense in an era of eroding values

Today, under the title Sleeperzzz, the station hosts friendly independent bunkhouse accommodation in a variety of charming converted vehicles – former sleeping cars and a delightful showman's wagon. Open March to end September. *Details www.sleeperzzz.com*

Railwayana

Like Lairg and Invershin (before it burned down), Rogart looks like a converted cottage – complete with dormers. Opened April 18 1868 by Sutherland Railway, closed June 13 1960 and then, surprisingly, re-opened nine months later on March 6 1961.

Passing loop at Rogart is one of longest in the North, a reflection perhaps of strategic position almost exactly half way between Inverness and Wick/Thurso.

Distances

Inverness 77 miles; Wick 85 miles; Thurso 77 miles.

Guidelines

Near the end of the Far North Line and in pretty sparse country. Passengers using this deserted station annually are numbered in the low hundreds. The figure might have been higher if nearby Halkirk station had been the one to remain open, but it closed in 1960, before even Dr Beeching could get round to finishing it off, presumably because of its close proximity to Georgemas Junction.

Hereabouts is the home of Caithness slate and the superb flagstones quarried locally and used nationwide for paving many streets and squares are also typically used as field dividers – and very attractive they are.

Railwayana

Opened July 28 1874 by Sutherland and Caithness Railway. Station house sold off by BR in 1988, renovated, then sold again in 1994 and further renovated for use as holiday accommodation with some occasional public access. A plaque on the station records that the property won the 1993 British Rail Premier Award in the Ian Allan Heritage Awards and that it was presented by none other than Sir Bob Reid!

Subsequently the property and some adjoining land was sold again and has since been occupied as a private house, with no public access.

Distances

Wick 21 miles; Georgemas Junction 7 miles; Forsinard 22 miles

SPEAN BRIDGE
PH34 4EP (Highland)

Guidelines
This is you back to civilisation after the long trek across Rannoch Moor. Hotel, 100 yards from the station. Next door, a general store/minimarket and just beyond a 'woollen mill', though quite what is actually milled there is uncertain. At one time you didn't need to leave the station itself to post a letter or to buy a pc: Spean Bridge PO stood right on the platform in a trim garden shed (*see picture left*).

Clever use of bus timetabling could open up all manner of travel options from here. Out on the main road, just opposite the hotel, is a bus stop from where, believe it or not, you can travel right through Skye to the Hebridean ferry terminal at Uig or alternatively take the stopping service to Inverness, or Glasgow!

The bridge, incidentally, from which Spean B. takes its name is by – who else? – Thomas Telford, and he only built it in 1819! How many of today's bridges will be standing in 2219?

Railwayana
Opened June 30 1891 by West Highland Railway and remarkably well preserved since then. A somewhat unfortunate brick and concrete signal box from a later date mars the scene, but the station buildings themselves have stood up well. There was for a long time even a delightful 'Have your ticket ready' sign from the early days of BR, executed in tasteful blue enamel.

It was from here on July 22 1903 that the ill-fated line to Fort Augustus opened. First closure came in 1906 when the extension to Fort Augustus pier closed, then in 1911 all traffic on the line came to a halt for lack of funds. The line re-opened in 1913 only to close again 20 years later on September 1 1933. Quite possibly the most disastrous railway of all time, it often grossed little more than £1000 a year. The track was lifted in 1946.

Distances
Glasgow, Queen Street 114 miles; Mallaig 51 miles; Fort William 9 miles; London, Euston 515 miles

STIRLING
FK8 1PF

Guidelines
Stirling and its castle is always a popular tourist destination. The station is well placed for the town and it's not too arduous a climb to the castle. An ambitious scheme entitled Stirling Futureworld once entertained all sorts of far out notions, including an astradome over the castle, and lifts going up the rock face. Needless to say, it never happened.

A less far-fetched scheme saw the old town jail get an imginative facelift and tourist information set up on the way up to the castle. Meanwhile The Smith Art Gallery has a stimulating and varied exhibition programme. Over by Bridge of Allan (you can get a bus there – or ride the line to B of A station) the MacRobert Centre on the university campus hosts theatre, music and film.

Railwayana
Opened 1847 by Scottish Central Railway and completely re-built 1912 by James Miller for the Caledonian Railway. Crow stepped gables and crenellations. Very interesting canopies and concourse. A late C.20 facelift enhanced the station, with some very fine woodwork and sensitive restoration of original detail.

Though most branch lines serving Stirling have long since closed, the station has not suffered the sorry fate of many others and indeed the line to Alloa has come alive once more. Busy commuter traffic to Glasgow, a regular service to Edinburgh, and through trains to Inverness and Aberdeen have all generated good revenue.

Towards the end of the BR era there was a Motorail terminal here which even boasted a day time service to Inverness – for those who couldn't face the A9!

Distances
Edin., Wav. 37 miles; Glasgow, Q. St. 29 miles; Inverness 152 miles; Aberdeen 125 miles; Euston 417 miles

Guidelines

From the size of the station one has to assume that Strathcarron has seen busier days. For a while in the 30s the LMS operated a bizarre 'motorail' service carrying cars from Strathcarron to Kyle to increase traffic on the Kyleakin car ferry.

The station is not small, but round about it, apart from the hotel, there is really precious little else. Loch Carron is several miles away on the other side of the loch. A local bus service runs from the station as far as Torridon but be sure to check: it's listed as once a day and not every day of the week – *(Details: DMK Motors 01520 722682).*

Nearer at hand, and within walking distance if you are hardy, is the Strathcarron Pottery. They do actually make it here and there is a restaurant as well. Most commendable local initiative.

Railwayana

Opened Dingwall & Skye Railway, August 10 1870. Main building (ignoring hideous modern windows) is original and of the Achnasheen pattern. Elegant iron footbridge – by the Rose Street Foundry, Inverness in 1906 – links the two platforms. The level crossing went through various permutations in the attempt to operate sans staff, dispensing eventually with gates as well.

Distances

Inverness 65 miles; Kyle of Lochalsh 18 miles

The one thing you won't find at Stromeferry is – you've guessed it – a ferry. A sign out on the main road makes that point clear. Time was when you could rely on a couple of hours' wait to cross the few hundred yards to take you into darkest Wester Ross. Now the road snakes around Lochcarron squeezing in beside the railway and always running the risk of closure from falling rocks. At one point taking refuge in a protective tunnel.

In its time the 'ferry has seen some changes. It was the first terminus of the Kyle line, before the money was there to get to Kyle; the home base for an extensive (and financially disastrous) shipping operation by the line's builders; a ghost village when the ferry ceased and boom town when the oil came.

The platform yard across the water at Loch Kishom was to be supplied by rail, hence a substantial investment in heavy dockside plant *(see top picture left)*. Even the hotel was taken over by the oil men. When the platform yard fell silent the railside yard was cleared *(see middle picture)* and then, tragically, fire destroyed the hotel – which still remained a charred ruin for years after.

Railwayana
Opened August 10 1870 by Dingwall and Skye Railway. Destroyed by fire (along with a 14-coach train) October 1891 and rebuilt. Strome pier demolished at the end of 1937. Station allowed to go into decline.

Distances
Inverness 72 miles; Kyle of Lochalsh 10 miles

Guidelines
It's always surprising to come across Tain. One has ceased to expect such ordered elegance. Station isn't all that central, but it's not far up the hill to main street – the outstanding Brown's Gallery, Tain Through Time interpretive centre and shops.

Meanwhile the station itself has undergone a spectacular and tasteful refurb, resulting in the creation of a spacious and comfortable café/bar *(pictured top left)* named, appropriately enough 'Station 1864' – see date of founding, below.

Not too strenuous a walk out of town to the renowned Glenmorangie single malt whisky distillery, with its ever-welcoming visitor centre and shop!

Railwayana
Opened by Inverness & Aberdeen Junction Railway June 1 1864. Low grey sandstone building, B listed, has a particularly pleasing aspect from the town side *(see picture bottom left)*. Entrance porch, complete with stone pilasters, and commodious stationmaster's house to the right *(advertised For Let when the photograph was taken)* give an overall impression of elegance, with an Italianate flavour.

Standard HR footbridge connects far platform and its simple shelter. Some fairly recent re-surfacing of platforms and approaches.

Distances
Inverness 44 miles; Wick 117 miles; Thurso 110 miles

Guidelines

Taynuilt is just a nice size of place for a casual visit and well placed for station. From nearby Taynuilt Pier (over the bridge) a mail boat service once plied on Loch Etive – alas no more. But worth looking out for, the old Bonawe iron works, relics of C18 industry.

Taynuilt will be remembered by lovers of Highland verse as birthplace (and last resting place) of the Bard of Tobermory, Angus Macintyre, the banker author of the much loved *Ceilidh Collection*.

Railwayana

Opened June 1 1880 by Callander and Oban Railway. Typical C & O pre-fabricated station, bearing date 1879. Until it was consumed by fire, Taynuilt stood as one of the unsung masterpieces of the Victorian age. Proof that such stations were really nailed together by Victorian joiners in white aprons is afforded by the existence in the Scottish Record Office in Edinburgh of photographs showing the very scene.

In its pre-bus shelter (and fire) days, Taynuilt boasted for many years a splendid locally manned bookstall. Alas, no more!

Distances

Glasgow, Q. St. 89 miles; Oban 13 miles.

THURSO
KW14 7DL (Highland)

Guidelines
Slightly out of town, but it's downhill all the way to the centre and Thurso is definitely worth a visit since it really is the end of the line – you can't go on. Town itself, (popn. all of 9,000!) has some splendid Georgian architecture. Houses with generous gardens front some of the streets, and destruction by 'improvers' has been kept to a minimum.

Search out the Caithness Horizons Museum (the former Town Hall) where is kept the extraordinary collection of flora (his 'herbarium') gathered by one time town baker Robert Dick. Circumstances had sadly obliged him to sell off his equally comprehensive collection of fossils to pay his bills.

Railwayana
Opened July 28 1874 by Sutherland & Caithness Railway, attempts by the Caithness Railway to build their own 21 mile link betwem Wick and Thurso, though authorised in 1866, having failed for lack of funds. Virtually identical in appearance to the terminus at Wick, though Thurso is of sandstone, while Wick is of Caithness flagstone.

Improvements in recent years have lifted the air of gloom which had fallen on Thurso station though sadly the station kiosk, with its stock of crisps, lemonade and sweeties, once much in demand with local school kids, is no longer.

For a number of years Thurso station sported a blue telephone kiosk, maintained by the local community council – quite a collector's item if you like that sort of thing *(see picture following page)*.

Distances
Inverness 154 miles; Georgemas Junction 7 miles.

Thurso

Not quite so remote, perhaps, as neighbours Corrour and Rannoch, but not exactly surrounded by bright lights. Station sign used to advertise 'Tulloch for Kingussie' pushing it rather, since Kingussie is a mere 30 miles away and well served by its own Highland line.

Railwayana

Opened June 30 1891 under name of Inverlair. Change-over came on Ne'er Day 1895. The well preserved 'Swiss' style brick and wood building has been put to welcome use as a bunkhouse, also serving moderately priced meals (*book in advance on www.stationlodge.co.uk.*)

In 1894 W. Highland entertained the crazy notion of driving a branch line past Loch Laggan to Kingussie. Luckily it came to nothing!

Two miles up the line towards Corrour was shortlived Fersit* station, opened August 1 1931 and closed four years later, in 1935.

Distances

Glasgow, Queen Street 105 miles; Mallaig 60 miles; Fort William 18 miles.

*(For an account of the narrow gauge railway built to link in with Fersit and serve the hydro workings, search out *The Lochaber Narrow Gauge Railway.)*

Shown left at Tulloch: 22 tonne engine block from derailed Class 66 loco, Loch Treigside, 2013.

'Where on earth am I?' This might well be your reaction when you disembark at the terminus of the 'new' Borders Railway. There is a settlement somewhere, but the new station is hardly at the heart of it. When the old Waverley line closed (courtesy the good Dr Beeching) it wasn't long before the developers moved in to the land around the elegant old abandoned Galashiels station. So when the time came to plan the new line it could hardly end in the middle of a retail park.

Hence nearby Galashiels 'station' is one of Scotrail's finest bus shelters (though there is a useful travel interchange across the road) and the line had to go on, across the Tweed to a brown field site in the middle of an industrial estate. The good news is you can share the red sandstone bridge across the Tweed with the line (see left) and enjoy a bracing two mile walk back to Gala and its shops and cafés.

Railwayana
Opened September 6 2015 by Her Maj. the Queen – who took the train to get there. As with all the other new stations on the line, modest provision has been made for the travelling public. The only substantial building on the site (seen below), helpfully marked Staff Only, is not going to win many architectural awards. The travelling public have to make do with a couple of bus shelters.

Short sighted track layout (as with the lack of sufficient passing loops on the line) has seriously hampered the provision of tourist steam excursions. A little forward planning and a (very) modest extra investment could have provided a turntable at the end of the line. As it is, there is not even provision for a steam loco to perform a run around. Poor show.

Distances
Edinburgh Waverley 35 miles; Stow 8 miles; Galashiels 2 miles

Guidelines

Surely the smallest community in Britain with the luxury of two railway stations – and both of them still open. Not only that, but Tyndrum has a lot else to offer, in season. Its position just where the road branches to Oban or Fort William and before the route divides for Stirling or Glasgow means it has an enormous throughput of tourist traffic during the summer – and the facilities to prove it.

If you are feeling energetic the West Highland Way goes right through the village – why not go with it north or south and pick up a train again at either Bridge of Orchy or Crianlarich?

Railwayana

Tyndrum opened August 3 1894 by West Highland Railway. Very well preserved example of the Swiss chalet style island platform station, not so long ago warmed by coal fires. In summer months well tended privet hedges and floral displays gave the traveller the misleadmg impression that he had arrived at a thriving Victorian spa. The 'Upper' was added on to the station sign on September 21 1953. Then in 1988 the order was reversed and the station became known as Upper Tyndrum.

Distances

Glasgow, Queen Street 64 miles; Mallaig 100 miles; Fort William 59 miles; London, Euston 466 miles

TYNDRUM LOWER

Opened August 1873 by Callander and Oban Railway. Present 'station' – what there is of it – opened May 1 1877. 'Lower' went on the sign February 28 1953, some seven months before Tyndrum got its 'Upper'! This must once have been the most basic stopping place on the whole system *(see picture bottom left)*. Wooden hut replaced by galvanised bus shelter *(see top picture – taken on a rare steam visit)*.

Distances

Glasgow, Queen Street 65 miles; Oban 37 miles.

Guidelines

This is classic 'doon the watter' holiday territory. Not perhaps as fashionable today as it once was, but still attractive enough for many folk. Not a few also commute between Rothesay on the Isle of Bute, just opposite, and Glasgow, passing daily through Wemyss Bay. Apart from the scheduled crossing to Rothesay, look out for other maritime excursions and, who knows, you might meet the paddle steamer 'Waverley'.

Railwayana

First opened March 1 1865 by Greenock and Wemyss Bay Railway. Present building, designed by James Miller and Donald Mathieson, dates from 1903. Spacious concourse and typical 'N' type roof girders are hallmarks of the Mathieson approach.

In many respects Wemyss Bay employs a scaled down version of the design philosophy applied with such success at Glasgow Central. Lessons learned on a visit to the US influenced Mathieson's approach to both stations. Façade on to the car park is the work of James Miller, who got the commissions for the railway hotels at Turnberry and Gleneagles. Bold, muscular Tudor revival, it is a visual delight. 'B' listed – for what it's worth!

Distances

Glasgow, Central 31 miles.

WICK
KW1 4QT (Highland)

Guidelines
If you're intent on reaching John o'Groats then you are probably better starting from Wick than Thurso. A Stagecoach service (No 77) should get you from Wick bus terminal to the Groat (and on to the Gill's Bay ferry terminal if you fancy a bargain trip to Orkney).

Wick itself doesn't have the attraction of neighbour Thurso. The harbour does absolutely nothing for the town – it could be such an asset. And the heart of the place is hard to discover. But there's always the Pulteney Distillery to visit.

Railwayana
Like Thurso, which it so much resembles, Wick station was given a facelift in the seventies with tasteful pine linings and the like. A wall plaque records the fact that 'Lady Jessamine Harmsworth' did the honours on June 14 1985 rather more than a
century since the place was inaugurated, on July 28 1874 by the Sutherland & Caithness Railway, a date set in stone by a carved relief plaque set in the outside wall *(see picture top left)*.

Wick and Thurso stations represent a rather successful attempt to get all the functions of a station under one roof.

Distances
Inverness 162 miles; Georgemas Junction 14 miles; Dingwall 143 miles.

And finally…

… no acount of the railway stations of Scotland would be complete without mention of the home base of the pioneering Scottish Railway Preservation Society at BO'NESS in West Lothian. Though strictly outwith the scope of this publication – the independent station is not on the main rail network – it merits a mention, not only as a vibrant rail centre in its own right, but as the source of many classic steam adventures. Seen above, a Railtours excursion crossing the Forth Bridge.